UEFA EURO 2020

THE OFFICIAL BOOK

Published in 2021 by Welbeck

Manufactured under licence by Welbeck. An Imprint of Welbeck Non-Fiction Limited, part of Welbeck Publishing Group

20 Mortimer Street London W1T 3JW

Editorial Director: Martin Corteel
Project Editor: Ross Hamilton
Design Manager: Luke Griffin
Design: RockJaw Creative, Eliana Holder
Picture Research: Paul Langan
Production: Rachel Burgess

The publisher has taken every reasonable step to ensure the accuracy of the facts contained herein at the time of going to press, but can take no responsibility for any incorrect information arising from changes that may take place after this point. For the latest information, please visit www.uefa.com/uefaeuro-2020.

A CIP catalogue record for this book is available from the British Library

ISBN 978-1-78739-403-2

Printed in Spain

10 9 8 7 6 5 4 3 2 1

FSC
www.fsc.org
MIX
From responsible sources
FSC® C009279

UEFA EURO 2020

THE OFFICIAL BOOK

KEIR RADNEDGE

CONTENTS

INTRODUCTION

UEFA EURO 2020 will be the most extraordinary in the tournament's history. It is being unrolled, after a year's postponement, in the shadow of the Covid-19 pandemic. Yet the rescheduling also offers a signal of hope and positivity to European football's worldwide audience.

This time there is no single host but a swathe of 12 footballing states in which a major city and venue will be eagerly awaiting their involvement. The pan-European party kicks off in Rome on 11 June and reaches a climax at the historic Wembley Stadium exactly one month later.

Tradition, the foundation of the world's most popular sport, has been evident at every step of the way. Frenchman Henri Delaunay had the dream of a European championship and provided much of the momentum that ultimately saw the creation of the European federation, UEFA, in the mid-1950s.

France played host to the inaugural finals in 1960, when the Soviet Union defeated Yugoslavia in the final at the old Parc des Princes in Paris. The 2020 finals celebrate the 60th anniversary of that first step in an appropriate manner and style: a EURO for Europe.

The European Championship's growth down the years has reflected its increasing popularity and the will of every European footballer to step out on the continent's grandest stage.

Initially the finals were contested between four teams, in two semi-finals, a third-place play-off and the final. In 1980, UEFA decided that more countries should be welcomed to the party, and doubled the complement to eight teams. A further 16 years on and England, in 1996, was the first host to boast a 16-team tournament.

The hallmark of the European Championship has been magnificent and dramatic football, so it was no wonder that more national associations wanted to share in the four-yearly festival. Hence the decision to expand the finals by an extra eight nations. France, five years ago, was the first nation to stage a 24-team tournament.

This expansion enlivened the qualifying competition, opening up the possibilities to many more members of the European football family. That vision has been extended further this time around, with the incorporation of the new UEFA Nations League in the qualifying system.

A majority of the previous winners of the crown will be duelling for new glory. This means the presence of record three-times title-holders Germany and Spain, twice winners France, as well as reigning champions Portugal and other fellow victorious nations Czech Republic (successor to Czechoslovakia), Denmark, Italy, Netherlands and Russia (successor to the Soviet Union). A footballing tour de force is promised for all who love the game.

As UEFA president Aleksander Čeferin says: "There is great pleasure in being able to bring EURO 2020 to so many countries and cities, to see football acting as a bridge between nations, and to carry the competition closer to the fans, who are the essential lifeblood of the game."

Below: The official adidas Uniforia match ball which will be used at EURO 2020.

Right: Portugal, led by captain Cristiano Ronaldo, won their first EURO title in 2016.

7

WELCOME TO UEFA EURO 2020

European football has never seen anything to match the innovative format drawn up for UEFA EURO 2020. Ever since the launch of the original Nations' Cup in the late 1950s, the central concept remained unaltered: a qualifying tournament followed by one or, at most, two countries hosting the finals. Not any more. The latest edition of the finals is a pan-European party with 12 countries sharing the festivities, the excitement and the drama.

A EURO FOR EUROPE

Expansion generated by popular success has marked the history of the UEFA European Championship ever since its first match in 1958. The number of participating nations has increased steadily and the finals have broadened from four teams, to eight, to 16 and then to 24 in France five years ago.

Now the finals of UEFA EURO 2020 are being spread far and wide between 12 cities representing 12 countries across the continent: 3,250km from Saint Petersburg in the north to Rome in the south and 4,300km from Bilbao in the west to Baku in the east.

Some 17 nations contested the first tournament. Nowadays all 55 members of the European federation can eye up a place at the final tournament. Their ultimate shared goal is pursuit of the Henri Delaunay trophy, named in memory of UEFA's original French general secretary, who was the driving force behind the competition's birth.

The dream of celebrating the finals' 60th anniversary with a one-off pan-European tournament was first set before the UEFA Executive Committee in Kyiv during UEFA EURO 2012. A positive sounding among member associations saw the proposal ratified in December of that year. In January 2015, a working group recommended that 12 cities should hold the group matches, with a 13th hosting both the semi-finals and the final. Ten of the 12 stadia should have a minimum capacity of 50,000, but at least two host venues could have lower capacities in order to give associations that would have never held EURO games the chance to do so.

By September 2013, no fewer than 32 countries had registered an interest. One year later, UEFA's Executive Committee decided on 12 cities to stage the group games and early knockout ties, with London's Wembley Stadium allocated the semi-finals and final. Each qualified host country should play a minimum of two group matches at

Left: Skillzy, a freestyle-loving character, was revealed in 2019 as the official mascot of UEFA EURO 2020.

The UEFA EURO 2020 hosts:
GROUP A: Rome and Baku
GROUP B: Saint Petersburg and Copenhagen
GROUP C: Amsterdam and Bucharest
GROUP D: London and Glasgow
GROUP E: Bilbao and Dublin
GROUP F: Munich and Budapest

Above: The host venues for UEFA EURO 2020 were announced with much fanfare in a ceremony in Geneva back in 2014.

home. Later refinements awarded Wembley with three group games and the Olimpico in Rome the opening match.

This is a far cry from the minimalist inaugural finals, which took place in France in 1960. These featured four teams, who played knockout semi-finals, the final and a third place match. That formula continued until 1980, when in Italy that year, the number of finalists was doubled to eight. They were divided into two groups of four. The group winners contested the final, with the runners-up meeting in what was the last third place play-off. In 1984, with the tournament back in France, two semi-finals were introduced after the group stage.

The steadily increasing popularity of the championship with players, officials, fans and media prompted further development when England played host in 1996. Simultaneously, UEFA's own membership grew sharply in numbers, after the accession to the European football family of the new nations that were created out of the former Soviet Union and Yugoslavia.

Thus, England's football summer of 1996 enjoyed the first 16-team finals, with four groups of four and then quarter-finals and semi-finals leading up to the final. The format was maintained when Belgium and Netherlands became the first co-hosts of the finals in 2000. Both tournaments also had the golden goal system decide the outcome in extra time in the finals: Germany defeating Czech Republic in 1996, and France overcoming Italy in 2000.

The positive experience of co-hosting encouraged more footballing neighbours to consider joint bids. Hence, Austria and Switzerland shared the staging of UEFA EURO 2008, then Poland and Ukraine in 2012. Four more years, and the complement of finalists rose to an unprecedented 24 sides in 2016, as the tournament returned to France for a third time.

UEFA EURO 2020 will also feature 24 teams and Dublin, one of the host cities, was the stage in December 2018 for the qualifying competition draw. This also brought formal confirmation from the UEFA president, Aleksander Čeferin, that a further entry route would be available to teams from the new UEFA Nations League.

One of Čeferin's first duties upon becoming president of UEFA in the autumn of 2016 was to launch the official tournament logo. The design shows multicoloured fan silhouettes standing either side of the competition's trophy on a green bridge, which is representative of the links between the host cities and countries.

As the UEFA president said: "UEFA wanted the 2020 tournament to be a true celebration of the game we all love and cherish. What better way could there be than to take the tournament, for one time only, to all four corners of our beautiful continent?"

The first goal in EURO history was scored by the Soviet Union's Anatoli Ilyin in a 3-1 win over Hungary in Moscow on 28 September 1958. Now who will write history of their own at Wembley on 11 July 2021?

THE VENUES

The UEFA European Championship has grown from its modest beginnings in 1958–60 into one of international sport's greatest and most popular showpieces. By the climax of the 2020 competition, the tournament finals will have been staged in 22 countries, including the current 12 venues: 11 will each host three group matches and one early-stage knockout tie, while Wembley also sees the two semi-finals and the final.

ROME
Olimpico in Rome

BAKU
Baku Olympic Stadium

SAINT PETERSBURG
Saint Petersburg Stadium

COPENHAGEN
Parken Stadium

AMSTERDAM
Johan Cruijff Arena

BUCHAREST
National Arena Bucharest

LONDON
Wembley Stadium

GLASGOW
Hampden Park

DUBLIN
Dublin Arena

BILBAO
San Mamés Stadium

MUNICH
Football Arena Munich

BUDAPEST
Puskás Aréna

Rome, Italy
OLIMPICO IN ROME

CAPACITY: 68,000
MATCHES: Group A: 11 June, 16 June, 20 June.
Quarter-final: 3 July.

Host to the opening game, the Olimpico was created in the Foro Italico sports complex in the Italian capital in 1953, ahead of the 1960 Rome Olympics. Since then it has been the shared home of Serie A clubs Roma and Lazio. The stadium is owned by the Italian National Olympic Committee and was rebuilt for the 1990 FIFA World Cup, when it hosted the final. Its four European club finals included, most recently, the 2009 UEFA Champions League final between Barcelona and Manchester United.

Baku, Azerbaijan
BAKU OLYMPIC STADIUM

CAPACITY: 69,000
MATCHES: Group A: 12 June, 16 June, 20 June.
Quarter-final: 3 July.

The Baku Olympic Stadium took over as the major international venue for Azerbaijani football from the old Tofiq Bahramov Republican Stadium, named after the former referee. The new venue was opened in 2015 in time for events at the inaugural European Games and to mark the 100th anniversary of the introduction of football to Azerbaijan. In 2019 it staged the UEFA Europa League final, in which Chelsea defeated Arsenal 4-1.

Saint Petersburg, Russia
SAINT PETERSBURG STADIUM

CAPACITY: 61,000
MATCHES: Group B: 12 June, 16 June, 21 June.
Quarter-final: 2 July.

The Saint Petersburg Stadium, on Krestovsky Island to the west of the city, replaced the old Sergey Kirov arena in time to play a central role in both the FIFA Confederations Cup in 2017, hosting the final, and World Cup, a year later. It has been hailed as one of the most technologically sophisticated sports arenas in Europe, and has a retractable roof. The arena, which is also used for concerts and other entertainment, is home to Zenit.

....

Copenhagen, Denmark
PARKEN STADIUM

CAPACITY: 38,000
MATCHES: Group B: 12 June, 17 June, 21 June.
Round of 16 (2D v 2E): 28 June.

The Parken Stadium is the most compact of the 12 UEFA EURO 2020 venues and is home not only to the Danish national team but also to FC København. Built in 1992, the stadium was constructed at a cost of €85m on the site of the 80-year-old Idraetsparken, which had been the Danish national team's traditional home. In 1994 it staged the UEFA Cup Winners' Cup final and then, in 2000, the UEFA Cup final. The stadium features a retractable roof, enabling access for up to 55,000 people at concerts held there.

....

Amsterdam, Netherlands
JOHAN CRUIJFF ARENA

CAPACITY: 54,000
MATCHES: Group C, 13 June, 17 June, 21 June. Round of 16 (2A v 2B): 26 June.

The Johan Cruijff ArenA has been home to AFC Ajax since its construction in 1996 and was the first stadium in Europe to boast a sliding roof. It has been remodelled ahead of the finals. In 2018 it was renamed after the legendary Dutch player and coach who had died two years earlier. The stadium, in the south-east of Amsterdam, hosted the 2013 UEFA Europa League final, in which Chelsea beat Benfica 2-1.

Bucharest, Romania
NATIONAL ARENA BUCHAREST

CAPACITY: 54,000
MATCHES: Group C: 13 June, 17 June, 21 June. Round of 16 (1F v 3A/B/C): 28 June.

The National Arena Bucharest was totally rebuilt and reopened in September 2011. The complex is named after Lia Manoliu, Romania's Olympic champion discus thrower at the Mexico Games in 1968. The opening match in the redeveloped venue was a goalless draw between Romania and France in a UEFA EURO 2012 qualifying tie. The next year the stadium welcomed the final of the UEFA Europa League, in which Club Atlético de Madrid beat Athletic Club 3-0.

London, England
WEMBLEY STADIUM

CAPACITY: 90,000
MATCHES: Group D: 13 June, 18 June, 22 June.
Round of 16 (1A v 2C): 26 June.
Semi-finals: 6 July, 7 July. Final: 11 July.

Wembley is one of football's most iconic venues, opened in 1923 with the legendary 'White Horse FA Cup final'. It hosted England's victory in the FIFA World Cup final in 1966 and the Olympic Games football finals in both 1948 and 2012, as well as the EURO '96 final and a host of major club events. The stadium was reopened in 2007 after a five-year reconstruction. The 315-metre arch is the world's longest single-roof span.

Glasgow, Scotland
HAMPDEN PARK

CAPACITY: 51,000
MATCHES: Group D: 14 June, 18 June, 22 June.
Round of 16 (1E v 3A/B/C/D): 29 June.

Hampden Park is the world's oldest international football venue. In 1937 a then record 149,415 saw Scotland play England. Hampden was redeveloped as an all-seater venue in 1992 and has continued to host internationals, domestic and European cup finals. These included the iconic 1960 European Cup final, in which Real Madrid beat Eintracht Frankfurt 7-3 and the 2002 UEFA Champions League final, which featured a remarkable goal by Zinédine Zidane for Real Madrid against Bayer Leverkusen.

Bilbao, Spain
SAN MAMÉS STADIUM

CAPACITY: 53,000
MATCHES: Group E: 14 June, 19 June, 23 June.
Round of 16 (1B v 3A/D/E/F): 27 June.

San Mamés is the traditional Basque home of Los Leones, the lions of Athletic Club. The original stadium was built in 1913, was a host venue at the FIFA World Cup in 1982, and then was rebuilt a century after its original construction. A statue at the entrance honours one of the home club's greatest heroes, Pichichi, whose name adorns the trophy awarded each season to the leading scorer in Spain's top league competition.

Dublin,
Republic of Ireland
DUBLIN ARENA

CAPACITY: 51,000
MATCHES: Group E: 14 June, 18 June, 23 June.
Round of 16 (1D v 2F): 29 June.

Dublin Arena was opened in 2010 after a total reconstruction of the original Lansdowne Road site, which had been a sports venue since 1872. The new stadium, like the old, hosts both elite football and rugby union. The first football international took place between Ireland and England in 1900. The new stadium, opened in 2010, hosted the UEFA Europa League final the following year, in which FC Porto beat Braga.

Munich, Germany
FOOTBALL ARENA MUNICH

CAPACITY: 70,000
MATCHES: Group F: 15 June, 19 June, 23 June.
Quarter-final: 2 July.

The home of FC Bayern München was opened in May 2005, when the record-breaking German champions moved over from the Olympic Stadium. One of its first major international occasions was the opening match of the FIFA World Cup in 2006, in which Germany beat Costa Rica 4-2. The stadium was the first in the world with technology to allow a full-colour change of the exterior illumination, which can be seen, on a clear night, from the Austrian Alps.

Budapest, Hungary
PUSKÁS ARÉNA

CAPACITY: 68,000
MATCHES: Group F: 15 June, 19 June, 23 June.
Round of 16 (1C v 3D/E/F): 27 June.

Hungary's new national stadium bears the name of Ferenc Puskás, the country's greatest player as well as a legend of the world game. The site was originally the Nepstadion (People's Stadium) which had been built in 1953 as a home for Hungary's Golden Team. This was demolished in 2016, when work began on the new arena. This is the newest of the UEFA EURO 2020 venues, having been opened in November 2019 with a friendly between Hungary and Uruguay, a repeat of their legendary FIFA World Cup semi-final from 1954.

MAGIC MOMENTS
Lev Yashin the first hero

Lev Yashin, the great Russian goalkeeper, was inspirational as the Soviet Union triumphed in the inaugural Nations' Cup in France. Yashin played all his career for FC Dynamo Moscow and made 74 appearances for the Soviet Union between 1954 and 1967. His agility and sharp reflexes guided the USSR to gold medal victory in the 1956 Olympic Games, to the quarter-finals on their FIFA World Cup debut in 1958 and then to European title glory in 1960 in France. Yashin was outstanding in the 3-0 victory over Czechoslovakia in the semi-finals in Marseille and again in the final defeat of Yugoslavia at the old Parc des Princes in Paris. The Soviets won 2-1, with an extra-time winning goal by centre-forward Viktor Ponedelnik.

FINAL
Soviet Union 2-1 (aet) Yugoslavia
Parc des Princes, Paris
10 July 1960

ROUTE TO THE FINALS

The expansion of the EURO finals to 24 teams from 16, first enacted for the 2016 tournament in France, has injected extra drama and excitement into the qualifying competition. The goal for the teams in the ten preliminary groups was a place in the top two slots, which guaranteed direct entry to the finals.

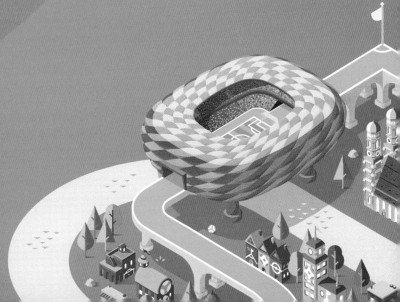

QUALIFYING STAGES

GROUP A

- 🟥 BULGARIA
- ◐ CZECH REPUBLIC
- ✚ ENGLAND
- 🔵 KOSOVO
- 🛡 MONTENEGRO

Right: Harry Kane

England vindicated their status as qualifying favourites while the Czech Republic and Kosovo jousted for the runners-up position. Manager Gareth Southgate's team thus followed up on the progress evident in reaching the semi-finals of both the 2018 FIFA World Cup and then the inaugural 2019 UEFA Nations League.

Centre-forward and captain Harry Kane was the 12-goal leading scorer in the entire qualifying competition for an England team who won seven of their eight games and lost only once, a 2-1 away defeat by the Czech Republic. They opened their campaign with a 5-0 defeat of the Czechs at Wembley and totalled 37 goals for a goal difference of +31.

The Czech Republic recovered from their early setback with victories over Bulgaria and Montenegro before losing 2-1 in Kosovo, who hit back for victory after conceding an early goal to Patrik Schick. The return, in November in Plzen, proved decisive. This time victory went to the Czechs by 2-1 and they finished in second place in the table with Kosovo third.

Simultaneously, England secured their place in the finals with a 7-0 victory over Montenegro. It was the perfect manner in which the Three Lions could celebrate the milestone of their 1,000th international. Kane contributed his third hat-trick for his country.

GROUP B

- ⚫ LITHUANIA
- ◐ LUXEMBOURG
- 🛡 PORTUGAL
- ◐ SERBIA
- 🔵 UKRAINE

Right: Cristiano Ronaldo

European champions Portugal were given immediate notice of the dangers awaiting them in their title defence as they were held goalless at home in their opening match by Ukraine. It was the first time the Portuguese had failed to score in 19 successive home matches. Goalkeeper Andriy Pyatov was the visitors' hero. The two teams eventually took the qualifying slots, with Ukraine completing the group undefeated to claim top place with Portugal runners-up.

The most persistent threat to both was provided by Serbia. They followed Ukraine's example by drawing away to Portugal, this time 1-1, on the second matchday. They even took a seven-minute lead through a Dušan Tadić penalty before Danilo rescued a point for the hosts.

Portugal finally regained winning form in their third outing with an important 4-2 victory in Serbia, which saw Cristiano Ronaldo open his scoring account in the tournament. Ronaldo scored in all Portugal's remaining five games. His goal in the concluding 2-0 win over Luxembourg, which secured Portugal's qualification, was his 99th for his country and made him the group's 11-goal leading scorer.

Luxembourg finished fourth largely thanks to a 2-1 comeback victory in their opening match against fifth-placed Lithuania, with goals from Leandro Barreiro Martins and Gerson Rodrigues.

GROUP C

- ⚫ BELARUS
- ⬛ ESTONIA
- ⬛ GERMANY
- ⬛ NETHERLANDS
- ✛ NORTHERN IRELAND

Right: Georginio Wijnaldum

The footballing rivalry of Germany and the Netherlands carried on from the UEFA Nations League into the European Championship qualifiers. The Netherlands took four points off the Germans to win their group in the 2019 Nations League, but the EURO qualifying competition was a different story. This time it was Joachim Löw's German team who finished top of the table with the Dutch as runners-up. The outcome of the group was dictated by Germany's opening 3-2 victory over the Netherlands in Amsterdam. Nico Schulz scored their last-minute winning goal.

The Netherlands later made amends with a 4-2 victory in Hamburg, but a goalless draw away to Northern Ireland denied them a chance of top spot. Germany celebrated qualification with a 6-1 victory over Northern Ireland in Frankfurt. Serge Gnabry scored a hat-trick to equal the great Gerd Müller's national team record of 13 goals in a calendar year.

Meanwhile, the Dutch were also celebrating a hat-trick, in their case from Georginio Wijnaldum, in marking their return to the finals with a 5-0 victory over fifth-placed Estonia. Gnabry and Wijnaldum were the group's eight-goal joint top scorers.

GROUP D

- ✚ DENMARK
- ✛ GEORGIA
- ⬛ GIBRALTAR
- ❚ REPUBLIC OF IRELAND
- ✚ SWITZERLAND

Right: Christian Eriksen

Denmark, European champions in 1992, completed their schedule undefeated. However points dropped in draws with Georgia, Switzerland and the Republic of Ireland (twice) meant they finished as runners-up to the Swiss. The Republic of Ireland earned a place in the play-offs via the Nations League, while Danish playmaker Christian Eriksen was the group's five-goal leading marksman.

The crucial match on which the outcome of the group turned was contested in its closing stages between Switzerland and the Republic of Ireland in Geneva. Mick McCarthy's Irishmen would have booked their place in the finals had they won in torrential rain. Instead one strike from Haris Seferović and an own goal by Shane Duffy lifted the Swiss back into the race and left the Irish needing to beat Denmark in their last game.

Denmark would have topped the group had they won in Dublin. Martin Braithwaite put Denmark ahead in the 73rd minute with Matt Doherty equalising ten minutes later. The 1-1 draw meant the Danes progressed as runners-up with the Irish third. Switzerland overtook Denmark to go top of the group by virtue of a 6-1 win in Gibraltar.

Georgia finished fourth with wins home and away over Gibraltar and draws against Denmark and the Republic of Ireland.

QUALIFYING STAGES

GROUP E

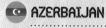 AZERBAIJAN

CROATIA

HUNGARY

SLOVAKIA

WALES

Right: Bruno Petković

Croatia, runners-up at the 2018 FIFA World Cup, maintained their reputation as a perennial contender by qualifying for the EURO finals in first place from Group E, closely pursued by Wales, Slovakia and Hungary.

The Croatians were inspired as ever by captain and playmaker Luka Modrić, and shared around their goals among group top scorer Bruno Petković (four), Ivan Perišić and Nikola Vlašić (three each). Crucially they lost only one of their eight matches, by 2-1 in Hungary.

A 3-1 victory over Slovakia in Rijeka in their last group game saw Croatia safely across the line. Defeat would have seen Slovakia leapfrog them, and left Croatia at the mercy of Wales or Hungary, but goals from Petković, Perišić and Vlašić proved decisive.

Wales hosted Hungary in their own last group game with direct qualification as runners-up the prize for the winners. The Welsh had reached the semi-finals in France in 2016 and can dream of a repeat after a 2-0 victory. The club pedigree of Gareth Bale and Aaron Ramsey, then with Real Madrid and Juventus respectively, proved too much for Hungary. Bale laid on the first-half opening goal for Ramsey, who struck again shortly after the interval. Hungary's consolation in defeat was a place in the play-offs.

GROUP F

FAROE ISLANDS

MALTA

NORWAY

ROMANIA

SPAIN

SWEDEN

Right: Claudiu Keşerü

Spain, champions of Europe a record-equalling three times, left no doubt about their quality in securing qualification with two matches to spare after a dramatic 1-1 draw against Sweden, who ultimately followed them through as runners-up, with Norway third and headed for the play-offs via the Nations League.

La Roja fell behind in Solna four minutes into the second half after a goal from Marcus Berg. They then lost goalkeeper David de Gea to injury and appeared on the brink of a first defeat until substitute Rodrigo fired through a crowded penalty area in stoppage time to rescue a vital point. Spain celebrated by scoring 12 goals without reply in their concluding outings against Malta and Romania.

Sweden had claimed the security of runners-up slot by following up the draw against Spain with a 2-0 win away to Romania. Berg again and Robin Quaison scored both goals in the first half in Bucharest. Both Sweden and Norway suffered only one defeat in the campaign but the Norwegians slipped up through having managed more draws (five) than wins (four). The Faroe Islands and Malta beat each other in their mutual home fixtures to finish fifth and sixth respectively, with the Faroese boasting a slightly superior head-to-head record. Romania's Claudiu Keşerü was the group's six-goal leading marksman.

GROUP G

 AUSTRIA

 ISRAEL

 LATVIA

NORTH
MACEDONIA

 POLAND

SLOVENIA

Right: Eran Zahavi

Poland and Austria reached the finals with decisive advantages over North Macedonia, which claimed third place on goal difference ahead of Slovenia. Israel finished fifth but claimed a significant consolation in the feats of striker Eran Zahavi. The veteran goalscorer, then of China's Guangzhou R&F, struck 11 times, which made him joint second-top marksman in the entire qualifying tournament. His tally included successive hat-tricks in victories at home to Austria and away to Latvia.

Poland reached the finals for the third time in their history with a frugal 18 goals in their 10 games. Six of those goals fell to captain and record marksman Robert Lewandowski. He failed to score in the 2-0 victory over North Macedonia, which took Poland through with two games to spare. Instead, Poland were fired to victory by second-half strikes from substitutes Przemysław Frankowski and Arkadiusz Milik.

Austria claimed the runners-up slot courtesy of a 2-1 victory over North Macedonia on the group's penultimate matchday. David Alaba and Stefan Lainer scored the goals. The North Macedonians took third place by winning their final tie 1-0 at home to Israel, having secured a play-off spot via the Nations League, while Slovenia lost out by going down 3-2 in Poland.

GROUP H

 ALBANIA

 ANDORRA

 FRANCE

 ICELAND

 MOLDOVA

 TURKEY

Right: Olivier Giroud

France followed up their victory in the FIFA World Cup in Russia by returning to the EURO finals in which they had finished runners-up in 2016. In fact, coach Didier Deschamps and his players were assured of qualification before their penultimate match, after pursuers Turkey and Iceland drew 0-0 shortly before Les Bleus kicked off against Moldova in the Stade de France in Saint-Denis.

France celebrated by winning 2-0 and concluded their programme with another 2-0 success in Albania, their eighth win in ten games. Chelsea centre-forward Olivier Giroud was the group's six-goal leading marksman.

Turkey returned to the finals for the fifth time in seven tournaments after a goalless draw at home to Iceland in the penultimate round. Iceland, surprise quarter-finalists in France in 2016, needed to win in Istanbul to overtake the Turkish. They staged a frantic finale only to be denied by the hosts' goalkeeper Mert Günok.

Andorra made history by ending their 21-year wait for a first EURO qualifying victory. They defeated Moldova 1-0 in the Estadi Nacional, despite having to play the last 35 minutes with ten men after a red card for Radu Gînsari. Andorra had lost all 56 of their previous qualifying ties since starting out against Armenia in September 1998. Marc Vales was their match-winning hero.

QUALIFYING STAGES

GROUP I

 BELGIUM

 CYPRUS

 KAZAKHSTAN

 RUSSIA

 SAN MARINO

 SCOTLAND

Right: Artem Dzyuba

Belgium's Red Devils became the first country to secure a place in the finals of UEFA EURO 2020 as centre-forward Romelu Lukaku scored twice in a 9-0 defeat of San Marino. Victory provided coach Roberto Martínez's side with an unassailable lead over all their pursuers. Nacer Chadli, Youri Tielemans, Christian Benteke, Yari Verschaeren (penalty), Timothy Castagne and two own goals completed the scoring.

Lukaku's double took his international tally to 51, becoming the first player to score 50 goals for Belgium, who ended the campaign with a 100 per cent record after scoring 40 goals and conceding a mere three. They finished six points clear of Russia and 15 ahead of third-placed Scotland.

Russia, quarter-finalists in hosting the FIFA World Cup in 2018, lost only twice – both times to Belgium. Their consolation was in reaching the finals for the fifth successive time and parading the group's nine-goal leading marksman in Artem Dzyuba.

The Russians ended Scotland's hopes of qualifying automatically by scoring four goals in 27 second-half minutes in Moscow for a 4-0 victory. Dzyuba (two), Magomed Ozdoyev and Aleksandr Golovin scored the goals that confirmed second-place qualification for coach Stanislas Cherchesov's men. Cyprus and Kazakhstan took fourth and fifth places ahead of San Marino.

GROUP J

 ARMENIA

 BOSNIA AND HERZEGOVINA

 FINLAND

 GREECE

 ITALY

 LIECHTENSTEIN

Right: Teemu Pukki

Italy approached the qualifying challenge as a team in a hurry. Goals from Nicolò Barella and Moise Kean provided a 2-0 win over Finland, and the Azzurri followed up by winning all their other nine games. They scored 37 goals and conceded just four to end the campaign 12 points ahead of Finland, who thus qualified for a major finals for the first time in their history.

Finland's hero was striker Teemu Pukki from England's Norwich City. Pukki's ten goals made him group top scorer and lifted him to third place in Finland's all-time national team ranking. They qualified with a game to spare after defeating Liechtenstein 3-0 in Helsinki. Jasse Tuominen and Pukki (two) struck the goals that ended a run of 32 unsuccessful qualifying campaigns for the EURO and FIFA World Cup. Prime Minister at the time, Antti Rinne, tweeted: "An incredible performance. Congratulations and thank you."

Finland had been pressed all the way by Greece as well as Bosnia and Herzegovina. The Greeks held on to third place in the group by defeating Finland 2-1 in their final game. Petros Mantalos and Kostas Galanopoulos scored the goals. Crucially, Greece drew 2-2 in Bosnia and then won the return 2-1 in Athens.

QUALIFYING COMPETITION TABLES

GROUP A

	P	W	D	L	F	A	Goal diff.	Pts
England	8	7	0	1	37	6	31	21
Czech Republic	8	5	0	3	13	11	2	15
Kosovo	8	3	2	3	13	16	-3	11
Bulgaria	8	1	3	4	6	17	-11	6
Montenegro	8	0	3	5	3	22	-19	3

GROUP B

	P	W	D	L	F	A	Goal diff.	Pts
Ukraine	8	6	2	0	17	4	13	20
Portugal	8	5	2	1	22	6	16	17
Serbia	8	4	2	2	17	17	0	14
Luxembourg	8	1	1	6	7	16	-9	4
Lithuania	8	0	1	7	5	25	-20	1

GROUP C

	P	W	D	L	F	A	Goal diff.	Pts
Germany	8	7	0	1	30	7	23	21
Netherlands	8	6	1	1	24	7	17	19
Northern Ireland	8	4	1	3	9	13	-4	13
Belarus	8	1	1	6	4	16	-12	4
Estonia	8	0	1	7	2	26	-24	1

GROUP D

	P	W	D	L	F	A	Goal diff.	Pts
Switzerland	8	5	2	1	19	6	13	17
Denmark	8	4	4	0	23	6	17	16
Republic of Ireland	8	3	4	1	7	5	2	13
Georgia	8	2	2	4	7	11	-4	8
Gibraltar	8	0	0	8	3	31	-28	0

GROUP E

	P	W	D	L	F	A	Goal diff.	Pts
Croatia	8	5	2	1	17	7	10	17
Wales	8	4	2	2	10	6	4	14
Slovakia	8	4	1	3	13	11	2	13
Hungary	8	4	0	4	8	11	-3	12
Azerbaijan	8	0	1	7	5	18	-13	1

GROUP F

	P	W	D	L	F	A	Goal diff.	Pts
Spain	10	8	2	0	31	5	26	26
Sweden	10	6	3	1	23	9	14	21
Norway	10	4	5	1	19	11	8	17
Romania	10	4	2	4	17	15	2	14
Faroe Islands	10	1	0	9	4	30	-26	3
Malta	10	1	0	9	3	27	-24	3

GROUP G

	P	W	D	L	F	A	Goal diff.	Pts
Poland	10	8	1	1	18	5	13	25
Austria	10	6	1	3	19	9	10	19
North Macedonia	10	4	2	4	12	13	-1	14
Slovenia	10	4	2	4	16	11	5	14
Israel	10	3	2	5	16	18	-2	11
Latvia	10	1	0	9	3	28	-25	3

GROUP H

	P	W	D	L	F	A	Goal diff.	Pts
France	10	8	1	1	25	6	19	25
Turkey	10	7	2	1	18	3	15	23
Iceland	10	6	1	3	14	11	3	19
Albania	10	4	1	5	16	14	2	13
Andorra	10	1	1	8	3	20	-17	4
Moldova	10	1	0	9	4	26	-22	3

GROUP I

	P	W	D	L	F	A	Goal diff.	Pts
Belgium	10	10	0	0	40	3	37	30
Russia	10	8	0	2	33	8	25	24
Scotland	10	5	0	5	16	19	-3	15
Cyprus	10	3	1	6	15	20	-5	10
Kazakhstan	10	3	1	6	13	17	-4	10
San Marino	10	0	0	10	1	51	-50	0

GROUP J

	P	W	D	L	F	A	Goal diff.	Pts
Italy	10	10	0	0	37	4	33	30
Finland	10	6	0	4	16	10	6	18
Greece	10	4	2	4	12	14	-2	14
Bosnia and Herzegovina	10	4	1	5	20	17	3	13
Armenia	10	3	1	6	14	25	-11	10
Liechtenstein	10	0	2	8	2	31	-29	2

EURO 2020 PLAY-OFFS

Four nations – North Macedonia, Scotland, Slovakia and Hungary – owe their presence at UEFA EURO 2020 to success in a new-format play-off tournament. This followed a decision to extend the competitive drama of the qualifying competitions by involving the Nations League, which had been launched in 2018-19.

Some 20 nations had reached UEFA EURO 2020 after finishing first and second in their groups in the main qualifying competition. That left four places available for the highest-placed non-qualifiers from each of the four Nations League tiers: A, B, C and D. They were then matched in four direct elimination knockout paths.

This placed Iceland on Path A; Bosnia and Herzegovina, Slovakia, Republic of Ireland and Northern Ireland on Path B; Scotland, Norway and Serbia on Path C; and finally Georgia, North Macedonia, Kosovo and Belarus on Path D.

A further sorting to balance the groups was necessary since Path A had three slots available compared with one in Path C. Ultimately, this resulted in Bulgaria, Hungary and Romania joining Path A, while Israel joined Path C.

Originally the playoffs had been scheduled for the early spring of 2020 but the disruption caused by the Covid-19 pandemic forced postponements until October and November. Each section opened with two semi-finals in which the highest-placed team, according to the UEFA Nations League ranking, met the fourth-ranked team, while the second-ranked team met the third. The semi-finals were single-leg matches on 8 October, with the higher-ranked team granted home advantage. The winners met in one-off finals on November 12 to decide who continued on to the UEFA EURO 2020 finals.

The long-delayed action commenced in dramatic fashion. Three teams – Scotland, Northern Ireland and Slovakia – all progressed to their respective finals courtesy of penalty shootouts. Path A produced semi-final success for Iceland and Hungary. Iceland, surprise quarter-finalists at UEFA EURO 2016, defeated Romania 2-1 in Reykjavik with two goals from midfielder Gylfi Sigurdsson, while Hungary beat Bulgaria 3-1 in Sofia. That was the Hungarians' first win away to Bulgaria in 63 years.

Path B brought victory for Northern Ireland over Bosnia-Herzegovina by 4-3 in their shootout in Sarajevo after a 1-1 draw. However the Republic of Ireland enjoyed no such fortune. Stephen Kenny's men went down 4-2 on penalties against Slovakia after a goalless stalemate in Bratislava.

Path C saw Scotland defeat Israel 5-4 on penalties after a goalless extra-time draw in Glasgow, where goalkeeper David Marshall saved Eran Zahavi's opening effort for Israel. Serbia needed extra time to win the other semi-final 2-1 in Norway.

Path D brought Georgia a 1-0 victory over Belarus in Tbilisi with a penalty from Tornike Okriashvili. In the other tie, Kosovo's dream of reaching a first major finals, only four years after being welcomed into international football, ended with a 2-1 defeat away by neighbours North Macedonia.

The four finals were staged on November 12 in Budapest, Belgrade, Belfast and Tbilisi. Hungary won the Path A final in dramatic style in the new Puskás Arena in Budapest. Two goals in the last two minutes from substitute Loïc Négo and Dominik Szoboszlai secured the Magyars' escape to a 2-1 victory over Iceland. The visitors had led from the 11th minute through Sigurdsson.

Path B's showdown in Belfast ran into extra time before Slovakia defeated Northern Ireland 2-1. Slovakia struck early through Juraj Kucka then conceded late with a Milan Škriniar own goal. The hosts' Kyle Lafferty hit a post before extra time brought a 110th-minute winner from Michal Ďuriš.

Scotland, in Path C, progressed to the closing stages of a major senior tournament for the first time in 23 years after winning their second successive shootout. Goalkeeper Marshall was their hero again. His save from Aleksandar Mitrović secured a 5-4 success after a 1-1 extra-time draw. Earlier, a 90th-minute header from Luca Jović had matched Ryan Christie's strike to earn the extra half-hour.

In Path D, North Macedonia reached a major finals for the first time in their 27-year history after a second-half goal from 37-year-old Goran Pandev earned a 1-0 win away to Georgia. Pandev, his country's most capped player and all-time leading scorer, struck his historic 36th international goal in the 56th minute.

PATH A
8 October 2020

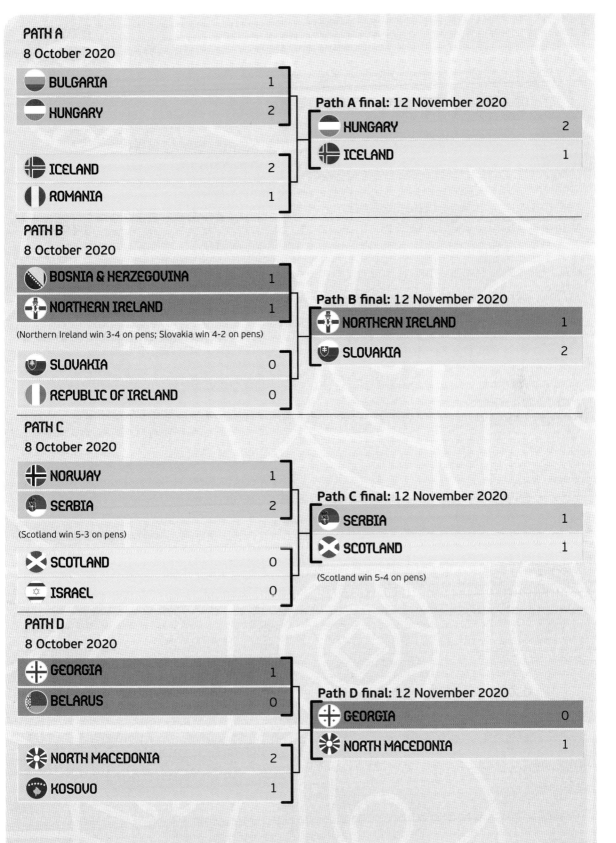

BULGARIA — 1
HUNGARY — 2

Path A final: 12 November 2020
HUNGARY — 2
ICELAND — 1

ICELAND — 2
ROMANIA — 1

PATH B
8 October 2020

BOSNIA & HERZEGOVINA — 1
NORTHERN IRELAND — 1

(Northern Ireland win 3-4 on pens; Slovakia win 4-2 on pens)

Path B final: 12 November 2020
NORTHERN IRELAND — 1
SLOVAKIA — 2

SLOVAKIA — 0
REPUBLIC OF IRELAND — 0

PATH C
8 October 2020

NORWAY — 1
SERBIA — 2

(Scotland win 5-3 on pens)

Path C final: 12 November 2020
SERBIA — 1
SCOTLAND — 1

SCOTLAND — 0
ISRAEL — 0

(Scotland win 5-4 on pens)

PATH D
8 October 2020

GEORGIA — 1
BELARUS — 0

Path D final: 12 November 2020
GEORGIA — 0
NORTH MACEDONIA — 1

NORTH MACEDONIA — 2
KOSOVO — 1

THE FINAL DRAW

The Romexpo in Bucharest, capital of Romania, provided the stage for the draw for the finals of UEFA EURO 2020. Coaches and senior officials of all the 20 qualified nations attended, as well as representatives of the 16 countries in the play-offs.

The process of placing the 24 nations who would contest the first European Championship spread across the continent was more complex than in the past. The top two teams in each qualifying group had been assured of their places in the finals, leaving four more to be decided by play-offs.

These play-offs were contested between 16 further countries split into four separate paths and based on their results in the 2018-19 UEFA Nations League. The mechanism was clear: each play-off path featured two single-leg semi-finals hosted by the countries who finished higher in the Nations League. The semi-final winners met in the final, with home advantage determined by a separate draw. Thus four further countries, still to be decided at the time of the draw, would join the direct qualifying nations.

Rome will host the opening match of the tournament, with the 1968 champions Italy playing Turkey on 11 June in Group A. The group is completed by Wales and Switzerland, with the other venue being Baku, Azerbaijan. Italy coach Roberto Mancini said: "We have a slight advantage by playing at home. Maybe some will think we are favourites but we need to confirm everything on the pitch, as always."

Wales reached the semi-finals five years ago and manager Ryan Giggs was satisfied with the starting point for the new campaign. He said: "We wanted to avoid playing Italy in Rome in the first game and we have done. Italy will be favourites then the rest of us are pretty competitive so we'll all probably be fighting for second place. We play them last game in Rome which is a tough one."

Denmark, Finland, Belgium and Russia were drawn together in Group B, whose matches will be staged in Copenhagen and Saint Petersburg. Denmark bring the status of having been champions in 1992, while Russia's Soviet Union predecessors were inaugural winners in 1960 and runners-up in both 1964 and 1988. By contrast Finland are appearing in the finals for the first time.

Belgium, third at the FIFA World Cup two years ago, were European runners-up in 1980 and coach Roberto Martínez said: "In terms of logistics, it's probably the hardest we could have had, playing Russia in Saint Petersburg in the first game and then Denmark in the second in Copenhagen, and then going back to Saint Petersburg." Russia coach Stanislav Cherchesov also sounded a note of caution. Cherchesov said: "We play the last match in the group in Denmark and against Denmark, so it could have been better. But no matter what the draw is we have to get prepared for each game and give our maximum."

Bucharest and Amsterdam will be the venues for Group C featuring the Netherlands, Austria, Ukraine and North Macedonia. The Dutch were absent from the finals in France in 2016 but have a proud record to defend as champions in 1988 and semi-finalists on three occasions.

Seven matches in the finals will be played at Wembley, which is an intriguing backdrop to England's participation. They have been drawn in Group D, which includes two of the teams to have beaten them in competition in the last two years in Croatia (at the FIFA World Cup) and the Czech Republic (in the EURO qualifiers). England manager Gareth Southgate said: "They are two teams we know and against whom we have had really good results and poor results. Croatia at Wembley is a brilliant opening game."

Wembley and Glasgow will each stage three group matches, with Wembley also due to host a second round tie, both semi-finals and the final. Making up Group D will be play-off winners Scotland, who will play two games in front of a home crowd at Hampden Park.

Three-time champions Spain, who will jointly host Group E in Bilbao with Dublin, play Sweden, Poland and play-off winners B, which turned out to be Slovakia.

Spain coach Luis Enrique said: "For me, Bilbao is one of the best stadiums in Europe alongside Wembley: it's marvellous, superb. I hope that we do not let people down. In a competition like this, you hope to play seven games and win them all."

Finally, defending champions Portugal and the last two world champions, France and Germany, were drawn together in Group F in Munich and Budapest. They will be joined by Hungary, winners in play-off path A. UEFA's decision to rank the teams according to their performance in the qualifying competition meant Portugal were among the third seeds, creating some tantalising fixtures in the group stage. Germany's coach, Joachim Löw, said: "This is a group of death. The expectations will be quite high. For our young team, this will be huge challenge but also a big motivation."

Below: Coaches, players and fans alike tuned in to watch the final draw take place in the glitzy Romexpo in Bucharest.

MAGIC MOMENTS
Panenka's iconic penalty

Antonin Panenka wrote his name into football folklore with the penalty that brought victory over holders West Germany in Belgrade. Czechoslovakia won a difficult qualifying group featuring England and Portugal, before a Panenka free-kick provided a crucial goal in a quarter-final victory over the Soviet Union. In the semi-finals he laid on a goal for Anton Ondruš in a 3-1 extra-time defeat of the Netherlands. The final against West Germany ended 2-2 after extra time and was thus the first to be decided by a shootout. Panenka stepped up to take the decisive kick with Czechoslovakia leading 4-3. Rather than blast the ball, he delicately chipped it over the diving Sepp Maier. Ever since, such a penalty has been known as a 'Panenka'.

FINAL
Czechoslovakia 2-2 (aet, pens) West Germany
Stadion Crvena zvezda, Belgrade
20 June 1976

MEET
THE TEAMS

One of the most fascinating aspects of the UEFA European Championship finals is the intrigue of the fixtures schedule cast up by the draw. Old rivals find themselves in direct competition once again, with a dramatic historical narrative created by great games and great players. But some of the teams will also be heading into the unknown, facing opponents they have mostly managed to avoid down the years.

GROUP A

Turkey and Italy, the 1968 European champions, are scheduled to kick off the entire footballing extravaganza at the Olimpico in Rome on 12 June. Wales and Switzerland wrap up Group A's opening matchday the next evening in Baku.

GROUP A

TURKEY

Turkey are back in the UEFA European Championship finals for the fifth time in seven tournaments since their debut in England in 1996. They reached the quarter-finals in 2000 and the semi-finals eight years later in Austria and Switzerland. Now they dream of emulating such progress under Şenol Güneş, the coach who took them to third place at the FIFA World Cup in 2002.

It took time for Turkey to establish themselves on the European stage. Despite a thriving domestic game, the national side missed out on qualification for the first nine editions of the EURO finals. Then, in the 1990s, everything changed. The national team began reaching tournament finals, Galatasaray and Fenerbahçe became consistent dangers in the European club competitions while developing magnificent training complexes back home.

Turkey's first club, Black Stocking, was formed at the turn of the century after English traders brought the game to the Ottoman Empire. A Turkish football federation was founded in 1923, months before the creation of the Turkish Republic. The national team's first taste of foreign competition came a year later at the Paris Olympic Games.

TURKEY AT THE UEFA EUROPEAN CHAMPIONSHIP

1960	Did not qualify
1964	Did not qualify
1968	Did not qualify
1972	Did not qualify
1976	Did not qualify
1980	Did not qualify
1984	Did not qualify
1988	Did not qualify
1992	Did not qualify
1996	Group stage
2000	Quarter-finals
2004	Did not qualify
2008	Semi-finals
2012	Did not qualify
2016	Group stage

COACH

ŞENOL GÜNEŞ

Şenol Güneş is an unusual national team coach at UEFA EURO 2020, having made his name as a goalkeeper. The experienced coach played 31 times for Turkey between 1975 and 1987 and earned a string of club honours, including six league titles and three national cups over a 15-year career with his hometown club Trabzonspor. He coached Beşiktaş and Bursaspor and in South Korea, but his greatest achievement was in a previous spell with the national team: he guided Turkey to a best-ever third place at the 2002 FIFA World Cup.

LEFT TO RIGHT: (Back) Mert Günok, Hasan Ali Kaldırım, Mahmut Tekdemir, Merih Demiral, Burak Yılmaz, Kaan Ayhan. (Front) Mehmet Zeki Çelik, Cengiz Ünder, Dorukhan Toköz, İrfan Kahveci, Kenan Karaman.

STAR PLAYER

CENK TOSUN

POSITION: **Striker**
CLUB: **Everton (ENG)**
AGE: **30**
BORN: **7 June 1991, Wetzler, Germany**
INTERNATIONAL DEBUT: **15 October 2013 v Netherlands**
CAPS: **45** · GOALS: **18**

Cenk Tosun provides a lively focus for Turkey's attack courtesy of club career experience garnered in Germany, where he was born, back in Turkey and now in England. He played in attack for Germany at Under-19 and Under-21 level, then committed to Turkey in time to make his senior debut in 2014 FIFA World Cup qualifying. He played twice for Turkey in the group stage of the finals at UEFA EURO 2016 in France. At club level, Tosun began with Eintracht Frankfurt before helping Turkey's Gaziantepspor win the national cup in 2012. He scored twice in their 3-1 victory over Orduspor. Subsequently he was sold to Beşiktaş then on to Everton in the English Premier League for £28m in January 2018. He moved to Crystal Palace on loan two years later, but returned in 2020.

Turkey won a place in the 1950 FIFA World Cup after beating Syria 7-0, but were unable to attend the finals in Brazil. They made it again in 1954, falling in the first round on their debut. A national championship was launched in 1960, attracting an increasing number of foreign players and coaches. In 2000, Galatasaray became the first Turkish club to win a European competition in the UEFA Cup. High-profile imported stars included Brazil goalkeeper Cláudio Taffarel and Romania playmaker Gheorghe Hagi.

The national team appeared at the European Championship finals for the first time in 1996, reached the quarter-finals in 2000 and then the semi-finals at both the FIFA World Cup in 2002 and UEFA EURO 2008. Turkey missed out on the next EURO finals in 2012 but returned to the group stage in France in 2016.

Qualifying Group H for UEFA EURO 2020 set up a testing proving ground for a rebuilt national team. Opposing the Turkish were the new FIFA World Cup holders, France, fast-improving Albania and the formidable Iceland side who had surprised the international establishment at both UEFA EURO 2016 and the 2018 FIFA World Cup.

A rising star in defence is Çağlar Söyüncü from Leicester City, who is expected to line up in the centre of a four-man back line. The midfield is run by the experienced Ozan Tufan, partnered by Hakan Çalhanoğlu of Milan, with strikers Burak Yılmaz and Cenk Tosun leading the line up front.

Turkey set off with victories over Albania, Moldova and France before losing 2-1 to Iceland in Reykjavik. Further victories followed before the crucial return against Iceland in Istanbul. The match ended in a goalless draw but that single point was sufficient to guarantee Turkey their ticket for the finals with a game to spare.

DID YOU KNOW?

Turkey conceded just three goals in their EURO 2020 qualifying campaign, the joint-meanest defence of any nation, along with Belgium.

GROUP A
ITALY

Italy have finished EURO runners-up twice since 2000 and are impatient to reclaim a title they have not won since playing host for the first time in 1968. The test for coach Roberto Mancini is to match the success he has achieved at home and abroad at club level.

Italy secured qualification for UEFA EURO 2020 with three matches to spare after a 2-0 win against Greece in Group J. Rome was an appropriate venue since the Stadio Olimpico will host the opening match in June.

Chelsea midfielder Jorginho put Italy ahead with a penalty after Andreas Bouchalakis handled a shot from Lorenzo Insigne and Juventus winger Federico Bernardeschi scored a second with ten minutes left.

Four times Italy have won the FIFA World Cup so they have plenty of ground to make up in the UEFA European Championship with only one title to their name. They have come close down the years. Italy were runners-up in 2000 and 2012, fourth in 1980 and 1988 as well as quarter-finalists in 2008 and 2016.

Both Italy's appearances in the final itself have been tense affairs.

In 1968 they defeated the former Yugoslavia 2-0 in a replay in Rome through goals from Luigi Riva and

COACH

ROBERTO MANCINI

Roberto Mancini is the latest in a long line of national team coaches who include Italian icons such as Vittorio Pozzo, Fulvio Bernardini, Enzo Bearzot, Giovanni Trapattoni and Dino Zoff. Mancini, 55, was an outstanding centre-forward with Bologna, Sampdoria and Lazio winning 13 major trophies. A further 13 trophies followed after he graduated into management with Fiorentina, Lazio, Internazionale, Manchester City and Galatasaray. Mancini succeeded Luigi Di Biagio after the Azzurri did not qualify for the 2018 FIFA World Cup finals.

LEFT TO RIGHT: (Back) Leonardo Bonucci, Gianluigi Donnarumma, Ciro Immobile, Francesco Acerbi, Lorenzo Pellegrini, Emerson Palmieri. (Front) Armando Izzo, Federico Chiesa, Nicolò Barella, Jorginho, Stefano Sensi.

JORGINHO

POSITION: Midfield
CLUB: Chelsea (ENG)
AGE: 29
BORN: 20 December 1991, Imbituba, Brazil
INTERNATIONAL DEBUT: 24 March 2016 v Spain
CAPS: 27 · **GOALS:** 5

Jorginho, full name Jorge Luiz Frello Filho, was born in Brazil but moved to Italy with Verona at 15. After eight years he joined Napoli where he became a key figure under coach Maurizio Sarri. Success in both the domestic cup and super cup prompted a transfer in 2018 to English Premier League club Chelsea with whom UEFA Europa League glory followed a year later. Jorginho qualified to play for both Brazil and Italy, the latter through his grandfather. In 2014 he opted for the Azzurri and made his senior international debut two years later. His fine form for both country and his club has secured his reputation as creative midfield anchor and penalty specialist.

Pietro Anastasi. In 2000 they were not so fortunate under the management of former goalkeeper-captain Dino Zoff. Italy were leading France 1-0 in stoppage time after the end of the 90 minutes when Sylvain Wiltord pounced for an equaliser. The Italians were then beaten in extra time by a strike from David Trezeguet under the now-discarded golden goal rule.

Italy did reach the final again in 2012, only to be defeated 4-0 by Spain in Kyiv. Further international reverses followed. At the FIFA World Cup in 2014 they fell in the group stage, at UEFA EURO 2016 they were beaten in a penalty shootout by Germany in the quarter-finals and they failed to qualify at all for the 2018 World Cup.

The latter setback prompted the appointment of Roberto Mancini as national coach. His reign began in the UEFA Nations League with a 1-1 home draw against Poland and 1-0 defeat in Portugal who topped the group with Italy finishing as runners-up.

Then the competitive focus switched back to the EURO qualifying competition in which the renewed Azzurri raised their game with a run of seven successive victories over Finland (twice), Liechtenstein, Bosnia & Herzegovina, Armenia and – decisively – Greece (twice).

A new-look Italy featured a mix of youth and experience from the young Milan goalkeeper Gianluigi 'Gigio' Donnarumma to veteran central defender and captain Leonardo Bonucci. In midfield Chelsea's Jorginho has been providing the platform for creative forces such as Marco Verratti from French champions Paris Saint-Germain and Napoli captain Lorenzo Insigne.

The evidence from the qualifying campaign is that they can also share the goalscoring duties with Lazio's Ciro Immobile and Torino's Andrea Belotti while much is expected of Federico Chiesa, son of a former Italian international forward, who starred at the UEFA European Under-21 Championship in 2019.

DID YOU KNOW?

Italy's win against Liechtenstein in March 2019 was their first 6-0 success in 57 years. They had previously beaten Turkey by the same margin in 1962.

GROUP A
WALES

Wales have become regulars at the elite level of European national team football. They return to the EURO finals having made their debut five years ago in France. Then, under Chris Coleman, Wales reached the semi-finals. Now a team managed by Ryan Giggs and starring Gareth Bale and Aaron Ramsey dream of another exciting adventure ahead of them.

Qualification, secured with a last-game victory over Hungary, has been a vindication for not only Giggs and his players but for the building work undertaken by previous managers John Toshack, Gary Speed – who died tragically at 46 in 2011 – and Coleman.

The present team embodies the spirit demonstrated by the national team ever since the creation of the Football Association of Wales in 1876, the world's third-oldest FA. The legendary Billy Meredith led Wales to six British Home Championship successes in the inter-war years. In 1927 Cardiff City, famously, became the only club ever to take the FA Cup out of England after a Wembley victory over favourites Arsenal.

In the 1950s new heroes emerged, most notably John Charles. The 'Gentle Giant' from Juventus led Wales to the last eight at the FIFA World Cup in Sweden in 1958. Other stars back then included Tottenham wingers Cliff Jones and Terry Medwin, Newcastle inside-left Ivor Allchurch and Arsenal goalkeeper

WALES AT THE UEFA EUROPEAN CHAMPIONSHIP

1960	Did not enter
1964	Did not qualify
1968	Did not qualify
1972	Did not qualify
1976	Did not qualify
1980	Did not qualify
1984	Did not qualify
1988	Did not qualify
1992	Did not qualify
1996	Did not qualify
2000	Did not qualify
2004	Did not qualify
2008	Did not qualify
2012	Did not qualify
2016	Semi-finals

COACH

RYAN GIGGS

Ryan Giggs hailed Wales' qualification for the UEFA EURO 2020 finals as among the great achievements of his life. That was an impressive statement from a man who had won everything in a 23-year playing career with Manchester United. He also captained Great Britain at the 2012 London Olympic Games. Giggs played 64 times for Wales between 1991 and 2007 before retiring in 2014. He had a spell as interim, then assistant manager of United before being appointed by the FA of Wales to succeed Chris Coleman in January 2018.

LEFT TO RIGHT: (Back) Wayne Hennessey, Daniel James, Chris Mepham, Kieffer Moore. (Front) Aaron Ramsey, Connor Roberts, Ben Davies, Gareth Bale, Joe Allen, Joe Morrell, Tom Lockyer.

STAR PLAYER

AARON RAMSEY

POSITION: **Midfielder**
CLUB: **Juventus (ITA)**
AGE: **30**
BORN: **26 December 1990, Caerphilly, Wales**
INTERNATIONAL DEBUT: **19 November 2008 v Denmark**
CAPS: **61** · GOALS: **16**

Aaron Ramsey demonstrated his class by marking his first start in a year with the two goals which beat Hungary in Cardiff in November 2019 to send Wales to the finals of UEFA EURO 2020. Over the previous year, injuries had hampered the box-to-box midfielder who began his career in South Wales with Cardiff City. At 17 he was an FA Cup finalist and his potential earned a £5m move to Arsenal. Ramsey scored winning goals in two further cup finals with the Gunners before joining Italian champions Juventus in the summer of 2019. Ramsey made his full international debut for Wales in 2008 and was a member of the team who reached the semi-finals of UEFA EURO 2016. He is among Wales' top ten all-time marksmen.

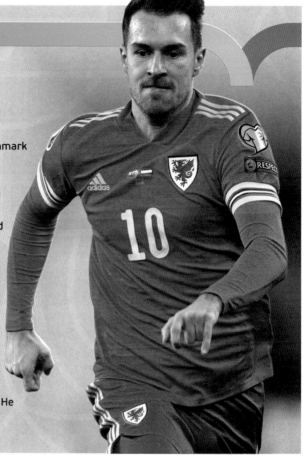

Jack Kelsey. That was the first time Wales had reached a major finals and the last, until the EURO campaign 58 years later in France.

Further fine players emerged down the years, such as Giggs, along with Liverpool centre-forward Ian Rush and Manchester United's Mark Hughes. Yet Wales failed narrowly to reach the finals of the FIFA World Cup in 1994 and were disappointed to miss out on an appearance at EURO '96 just across the border in England.

Hughes took over as manager in the spring of 2000 and again suffered a near miss. Wales reached the qualifying play-offs for EURO 2004 but lost 1-0 to Russia. The 2008 and 2012 campaigns brought further disappointments before Wales finally broke through to join

the elite in 2016. The squad in France was built around the likes of Ramsey, Gareth Bale, Ashley Williams, Joe Allen and Wayne Hennessey, who had all been promoted by Toshack during his managerial spell between 2005 and 2010.

In winger Bale, Wales boast one of the most exciting footballers in Europe. He has always remained intensely committed to the Welsh cause, which he leads both by example and as captain. Yet the emergence of more players to share the attacking burden was illustrated by the fact that Bale scored only two goals in the last qualifying competition.

Group E saw Wales matched against Azerbaijan, Croatia, Hungary and Slovakia. They began with a

1-0 victory over Slovakia then lost to both Croatia, runners-up in the 2018 FIFA World Cup, and Hungary. But those were their last defeats. A five-game unbeaten run, crowned by a 2-0 home victory over the Hungarians, secured qualification for Wales in second place, pipping Slovakia by one point.

DID YOU KNOW?

Founded in 1876, the Football Association of Wales is the third oldest national association in world football, behind England (1863) and Scotland (1873).

GROUP A
SWITZERLAND

Switzerland progressed beyond the EURO finals group stage for the first time in France five years ago. They will be hoping to emulate that performance this time around. Coach Vladimir Petković has built effectively on the work of his retired predecessor Ottmar Hitzfeld and will bring to the finals a squad heavy in tournament experience.

They qualified for a share of the limelight by finishing on top of Group D ahead of Denmark, the Republic of Ireland, Georgia and Gibraltar. Their 19 goals were shared around. The 24-year-old centre-forward Cedric Itten was their leading marksman. He scored three, followed by midfielders Granit Xhaka and Denis Zakaria with two each.

Switzerland opened with a 2-0 win in Georgia and were then held 3-3 at home by Denmark after conceding two goals in the last five minutes. The return against Denmark resulted in a 1-0 defeat. Before the ties of the last matchday, Switzerland's qualification status from a three-way duel with Denmark and the Republic of Ireland hung in the balance. They ensured top place in the table by winning 6-1 in Gibraltar, while the Irish and Danes drew 1-1 in Dublin. Itten scored twice on only his second international appearance.

LEFT TO RIGHT: (Back) Denis Zakaria, Kevin Mbabu, Ricardo Rodríguez, Nico Elvedi, Manuel Akanji, Granit Xhaka, Yann Sommer. (Front) Steven Zuber, Remo Freuler, Albian Ajeti, Breel Embolo.

SWITZERLAND AT THE UEFA EUROPEAN CHAMPIONSHIP

1960	Did not qualify
1964	Did not qualify
1968	Did not qualify
1972	Did not qualify
1976	Did not qualify
1980	Did not qualify
1984	Did not qualify
1988	Did not qualify
1992	Did not qualify
1996	Group stage
2000	Did not qualify
2004	Group stage
2008	Group stage
2012	Did not qualify
2016	Round of 16

COACH

VLADIMIR PETKOVIĆ

Vladimir Petković had a difficult act to follow in the retired Ottmar Hitzfeld, whom he succeeded after Switzerland had reached the second round of the 2014 FIFA World Cup. His initial task was accomplished as he led Switzerland to the round of 16 at UEFA EURO 2016. Born in Sarajevo, Petković had played in midfield for a dozen clubs in the former Yugoslavia and Switzerland. He coached his old club Bellinzona before moving on to Young Boys and FC Sion, Samsunspor in Turkey and Italy's Lazio, with whom he won the Coppa Italia.

STAR PLAYER

YANN SOMMER

POSITION: **Goalkeeper**
CLUB: **VfL Borussia Mönchengladbach (GER)**
AGE: **32**
BORN: **17 December 1988, Morges, Switzerland**
INTERNATIONAL DEBUT: **30 May 2012 v Romania**
CAPS: **58** · GOALS: **0**

Yann Sommer made his name, with his sharp reflexes and goal-area command, in a seven-year spell during which he helped Basel win four league titles and the Swiss Cup once. He also spent time on loan to Grasshopper Club Zürich, as well as with FC Vaduz in neighbouring Liechtenstein. Sommer played for Switzerland at all youth levels and was a UEFA European Under-21 Championship runner-up in 2011. In 2014 he was a member of the senior squad at the FIFA World Cup and then transferred to the German Bundesliga with Borussia Mönchengladbach. Two years later he was promoted to first choice for Switzerland in their run to the knockout stages of UEFA EURO 2016 in France and also in the subsequent World Cup in 2018 in Russia.

Switzerland have always been at the forefront of world football without ever actually winning anything at senior level, because both UEFA and world governing body FIFA are headquartered in the country.

An historic British influence is evident in the names of clubs such as Grasshopper Club Zürich and Young Boys, though no Swiss side has ever reached the final of a European competition. The national side, however, have fared better, particularly in the 1920s and 1930s. They were runners-up in the 1924 Olympic Games and quarter-finalists at both the 1934 and 1938 FIFA World Cups.

The most famous names of this era were the Abegglen brothers, Max and André, who scored more than 60 goals between them. The man responsible for this success was Karl Rappan, the 'father' of Swiss football. He guided Switzerland to the finals of four of the first five World Cups played after the Second World War. Their best performance was in 1954 when, as hosts, they reached the quarter-finals.

After 1966, the national side suffered a reversal of fortunes and failed to qualify for anything until returning to the FIFA World Cup in 1994 under English manager Roy Hodgson. They made their EURO finals debut two years later. Since 2004 Switzerland have been missing from the finals of the two major national team tournaments only once, the European finals in 2012.

Yann Sommer has been Switzerland's No1 goalkeeper for the past six years behind a defence leaning on Milan's Ricardo Rodríguez and Fabian Schär of Newcastle United. The full-back has played more than 50 times for Switzerland since his debut in 2013. Captain Granit Xhaka is their most experienced midfielder, while Haris Seferović has been leading the Swiss attack for the past eight years.

The challenge now is to put all that experience to work.

DID YOU KNOW?

Switzerland have successfully negotiated every group stage under Petković but are yet to win a knockout match: at the 2014 and 2018 FIFA World Cups, EURO 2016 and the UEFA Nations League.

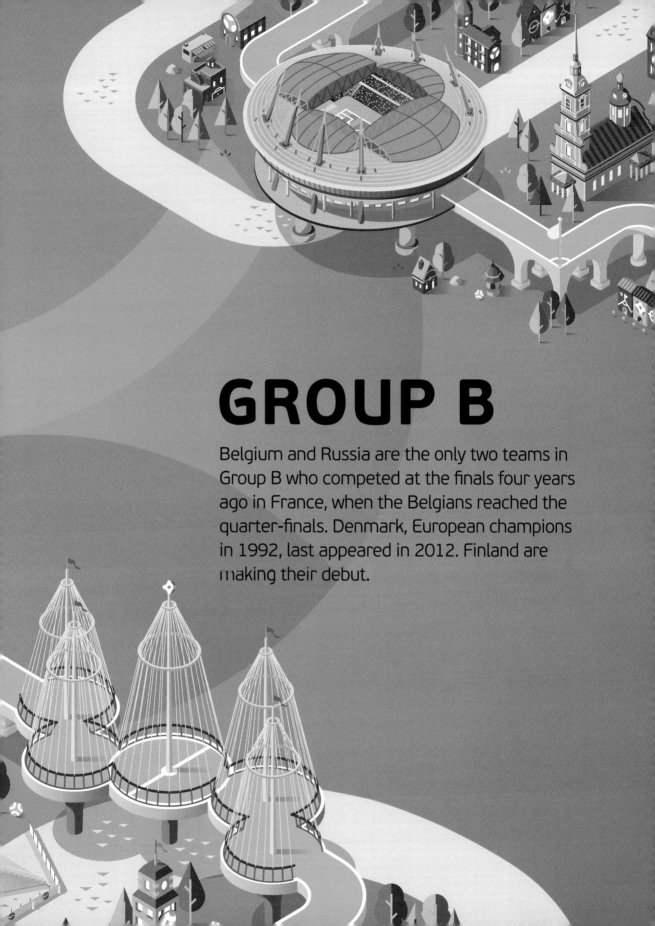

GROUP B

Belgium and Russia are the only two teams in Group B who competed at the finals four years ago in France, when the Belgians reached the quarter-finals. Denmark, European champions in 1992, last appeared in 2012. Finland are making their debut.

GROUP B
DENMARK

Denmark are welcome back at the EURO finals after being absent in 2016. A new generation of players will hope to follow in the footsteps of the Danish sides that lit up major finals between 1984 and 2004, most notably the revered European Championship-winning team. They were dealt a tough hand on their last appearance eight years ago – having been drawn with Germany, the Netherlands and Portugal – and could not progress from their group.

The Danes were among the first countries in continental Europe to take up football and boast some of the oldest clubs in the world. They enjoyed their greatest early success at the Olympic Games. Denmark were winners in the 1906 Intercalated Games and runners-up in 1908 and 1912, when they produced some outstanding footballers including Nils Middelboe, who would play with success in England with Chelsea.

A period of decline occurred during the inter-war years before qualification for the 1948 and 1960 Olympics sparked a brief revival. But the amateur nature of the domestic game, together with a rule that barred foreign-based players from the national side, delayed further progress.

The 1970s prompted a significant change. A flood of outstanding players – led by 1977 European Footballer of the Year Allan Simonsen

DENMARK AT THE UEFA EUROPEAN CHAMPIONSHIP

1960	Did not qualify
1964	Fourth place
1968	Did not qualify
1972	Did not qualify
1976	Did not qualify
1980	Did not qualify
1984	Semi-finals
1988	Group stage
1992	WINNERS
1996	Group stage
2000	Group stage
2004	Group stage
2008	Did not qualify
2012	Group stage
2016	Did not qualify

COACH

ÅGE HAREIDE

Åge Hareide, born on 23 September 1953, is a former Norway international defender who has been national manager of Denmark since 2015. Hareide played 50 times for his country during a 17-year club career with Hoødd and Molde in Norway, as well as with Manchester City and Norwich City in England. Hareide found instant success as a club coach. He won league titles in Sweden with Helsingborg and Malmö, in Denmark with Brøndby as well as back home with Rosenborg. He was also manager of Norway from 2003 to 2008.

LEFT TO RIGHT: (Back) Kasper Schmeichel, Yussuf Poulsen, Henrik Dalsgaard, Andreas Christensen, Simon Kjær, Nicolai Jørgensen. (Front) Lasse Schöne, Martin Braithwaite, Jens Stryger Larsen, Thomas Delaney, Christian Eriksen.

STAR PLAYER

KASPER SCHMEICHEL

POSITION: Goalkeeper
CLUB: Leicester City (ENG)
AGE: 34
BORN: 5 November 1986, Copenhagen, Denmark
INTERNATIONAL DEBUT: 3 February 2016 v FYR Macedonia
CAPS: 60 • GOALS: 0

Kasper Schmeichel's success with the Danish national team and at club level have fulfilled a certain destiny for the son of Peter Schmeichel, who kept goal for their country on 129 occasions between 1987 and 2001. Kasper has since established himself as an outstanding player in his own right in a 15-year career. He began with Manchester City, had a number of spells on loan, before joining Notts County, Leeds United then Leicester City in 2011. Schmeichel was outstanding in the club's historic Premier League triumph in 2016. He has been hailed twice as Danish footballer of the year after winning more than 50 caps. At the 2018 FIFA World Cup he surpassed his father's record of 533 minutes unbeaten for Denmark.

– left Denmark to play abroad. This promoted an end in 1976 to the ban on 'exiles' such as Michael Laudrup, Preben Elkjær, Jesper Olsen, Morten Olsen and Søren Lerby playing from the national side. The result was dramatic. Suddenly Denmark became a power again on the international stage.

These players and other new stars formed the nucleus of the team who reached the semi-finals of the 1984 EURO in France and round of 16 at the FIFA World Cup in Mexico two years later.

In the late 1980s the league was restructured, and a new generation of players – including Michael Laudrup's brother, Brian – emerged to propel Denmark to the dizzying heights of European champions in 1992. That unexpected success in Sweden was all the more remarkable as Denmark had been last-minute replacements for Yugoslavia.

Subsequently Denmark reached the finals of both the FIFA World Cup and the UEFA European Championship on four occasions each, but without ever progressing beyond the quarter-finals again.

Reviving hope for UEFA EURO 2020 has been a team built around the experience of Kasper Schmeichel in goal, Simon Kjær in defence, Christian Eriksen, Lasse Schöne and Thomas Delaney in midfield plus Yussuf Poulsen, Martin Braithwaite and Nicolai Jørgensen in attack.

Denmark were drawn in qualifying Group D with Georgia, Gibraltar, Republic of Ireland and favourites Switzerland. They opened their campaign with draws against Switzerland and the Irish, then hit their stride with a 5-1 defeat of Georgia. In the closing stages, Åge Hareide's men won 1-0 at home to Switzerland with a late goal from Poulsen. That victory offered a chance to finish top of the group, but Denmark were held 1-1 in Dublin in their last game, and ended one point behind the Swiss in second place. Eriksen was the group's five-goal top scorer.

DID YOU KNOW?

Father and son goalkeepers Peter and Kasper Schmeichel have amassed more than 180 international caps between them for Denmark.

GROUP B
FINLAND

Finland are making their EURO finals debut after a remarkable qualifying campaign. The national team's emergence among the elite is guaranteed to accelerate the enthusiasm of football in a country where winter snow sports are more dominant. It is a remarkable story for a nation whose team stood 110th in the world rankings only four years ago.

Yet football is no stranger to Finland. English businessmen and workers imported the game in 1890, initially in the capital, Helsinki. The Football Association of Finland was founded in 1907 and the creation of a national championship followed a year later. In 1911 Finland played their first international, losing 5-2 at home to neighbours Sweden.

Finland were also quickly into the international competitive arena, playing at the 1912 Olympic Games in Stockholm, albeit without success. Until now the national side had never reached the finals of the FIFA World Cup or EURO and none of their clubs had ever progressed beyond the quarter-finals of any of the European competitions.

The challenge of the northern climate has seen most of Finland's finest footballers go abroad to turn professional, notably with

LEFT TO RIGHT: (Back) Tim Sparv, Lukáš Hrádecký, Paulus Arajuuri, Joona Toivio, Kasper Hämäläinen, Sauli Väisänen. (Front) Robin Lod, Teemu Pukki, Glen Kamara, Juha Pirinen, Mikael Granlund.

FINLAND AT THE UEFA EUROPEAN CHAMPIONSHIP

1960	Did not enter
1964	Did not enter
1968	Did not qualify
1972	Did not qualify
1976	Did not qualify
1980	Did not qualify
1984	Did not qualify
1988	Did not qualify
1992	Did not qualify
1996	Did not qualify
2000	Did not qualify
2004	Did not qualify
2008	Did not qualify
2012	Did not qualify
2016	Did not qualify

COACH

MARKKU KANERVA

Markku Kanerva had undertaken two spells as caretaker coach of the Finland national team and managed the Under-21s before being appointed in his own right to succeed Hans Backe in 2016. The task of improving results was a challenging one since Finland had just gone 13 games without a win, but the former international and HJK Helsinki defender gradually turned the team around. Not only did he guide Finland to the EURO finals for the first time, he also led them to promotion from their group in the 2018/19 UEFA Nations League.

TEEMU PUKKI

POSITION: **Striker**
CLUB: **Norwich City (ENG)**
AGE: **31**
BORN: **29 March 1990, Kotka, Finland**
INTERNATIONAL DEBUT: **4 February 2009 v Japan**
CAPS: **87** · GOALS: **27**

Teemu Pukki is only a handful of goals away from overtaking Jari Litmanen as Finland's all-time top scorer. He has been leading his country's attack for the past decade and scored ten goals in the UEFA EURO 2020 qualifying campaign. Pukki began his career with hometown KTP Kotka, where he first earned selection for Finland at youth level. His eye for goal earned transfers not only at home to HJK Helsinki but abroad to Spain, Germany, Scotland and Denmark with Sevilla, Schalke 04, Celtic and Brøndby respectively. In 2018 Pukki moved to English football with Norwich City on a free transfer. He was top scorer in his first season with 29 goals, which shot them up briefly into the English Premier League.

clubs in Belgium, Germany and the Netherlands. The most successful export has been forward Jari Litmanen, who became, with Ajax in 1995, the first Finnish player to secure a UEFA Champions League winners medal.

His most noted professional predecessors were winger Juhani Peltonen and centre-back Arto Tolsa in the 1960s. Later, midfielder or central defender Kari Ukkonen spent more than a decade in Belgian football. Now the Finnish flag is being carried forward in the club game by the likes of free-scoring Teemu Pukki, with Norwich City in English football, German-based goalkeeper Lukáš Hrádecký (Bayer 04 Leverkusen), defender Jere Uronen (KRC Genk) as well as midfielder and national team captain

Tim Sparv who plays for AEL Larissa in Greece.

Finland's FA has looked to a number of foreign coaches down the years, including England's Roy Hodgson and Stuart Baxter as well as Richard Møller Nielsen, who led Denmark to victory at EURO '92. The most recent import was Sweden's Hans Backe in 2015. He was succeeded by former Finland international Markku Kanerva in time to confront a challenging six-team Group J in the 2020 qualifying competition. Their rivals were former European champions Italy and Greece, as well as Armenia, Bosnia and Herzegovina, and Liechtenstein.

The Italians ran away with the group, winning all of their ten matches, including victories at home and away over Finland. The Finns,

undaunted, finished 12 points behind Italy as group runners-up. Finland's most threatening challengers for second spot were Greece. Eventually Kanerva's men won six and lost four matches to end up with 18 points, four clear of the Greeks. Finland lost their last match to Greece, but by then the outcome of the group had already been decided.

DID YOU KNOW?

Prior to Finland's qualification, 33 of UEFA's 55 national association members have previously graced a EURO finals.

BELGIUM

Belgium have been one of the pillars of international football ever since the game's early years. All that remains is for such commitment to be sealed with a major prize. UEFA EURO 2020 provides an ideal opportunity to make up for the Red Devils' past near misses.

Progress to the finals was achieved from qualifying Group I with three matches to spare. A 9-0 victory over San Marino saw Belgium become the first team to qualify. Romelu Lukaku's two goals not only lifted his international tally to 51 but made him the first player to reach a half-century for Belgium.

The Belgian FA, founded in 1895, was one of the driving forces behind the formation of world federation FIFA and one of only four European nations to go to Uruguay for the first World Cup in 1930.

For years the amateur structure of the domestic game hindered progress in terms of results. After formal professionalism was approved in 1972, however, the international fortunes of both Belgium's clubs and national team soon improved.

Between 1972 and 1984 Belgium reached the last eight of four successive European

BELGIUM AT THE UEFA EUROPEAN CHAMPIONSHIP

1960	Did not enter
1964	Did not qualify
1968	Did not qualify
1972	Third place
1976	Did not qualify
1980	Runners-up
1984	Group stage
1988	Did not qualify
1992	Did not qualify
1996	Did not qualify
2000	Group stage
2004	Did not qualify
2008	Did not qualify
2012	Did not qualify
2016	Quarter-finals

COACH

ROBERTO MARTÍNEZ

Roberto Martínez is a former Spanish midfielder who has been in charge of Belgium since succeeding Marc Wilmots in 2016. Now 47, Martinez began his playing career at Real Zaragoza, with whom he won the Copa del Rey before moving to British football with Wigan Athletic, Motherwell, Walsall and Swansea City. Martinez began in management with Swansea and guided Wigan to FA Cup success before moving to Everton. He led Belgium's Red Devils to the EURO quarter-finals in 2016 then third place at the 2018 FIFA World Cup.

LEFT TO RIGHT: (Front) Toby Alderweireld, Youri Tielemans, Kevin De Bruyne, Thorgan Hazard, Eden Hazard. (Back) Thibaut Courtois, Romelu Lukaku, Axel Witsel, Thomas Meunier, Vincent Kompany, Jan Vertonghen.

KEVIN DE BRUYNE

POSITION: Midfield
CLUB: Manchester City (ENG)
AGE: 29
BORN: 28 June 1991, Ghent, Belgium
INTERNATIONAL DEBUT: 11 August 2010 v Finland
CAPS: 78 • GOALS: 20

Kevin De Bruyne has been at the creative heart of the achievements of Belgium and, at club level, Manchester City in the English Premier League over the past four years. Gifted with power and the eye for a defence-turning pass he made his Belgium debut in 2010 and was a key member of the squad who reached the closing stages of UEFA EURO 2016 and the FIFA World Cups in 2014 and 2018. De Bruyne was a Belgian league champion with Genk in 2011 and moved to Chelsea, Werder Bremen on loan and Wolfsburg before joining City for a then club record €70m in 2015. Since then he has won two Premier League titles, four League Cups and one FA Cup.

Championships. In Italy in 1980 a team coached by Guy Thys reached the final in Rome before losing 2-1 to West Germany and a last-minute goal from Horst Hrubesch.

The class of 1980 represented Belgium for almost a decade and contained many of the country's most celebrated players. These included goalkeeper Jean-Marie Pfaff, full-back Eric Gerets and 96-cap forward Jan Ceulemans. At the 1986 FIFA World Cup finals a team starring Enzo Scifo lost only to eventual champions Argentina in the semi-finals.

In 2000 Belgium made history, with the Netherlands, in staging the first co-hosted UEFA European Championship. A team led by Marc Wilmots and Emile Mpenza opened with a victory over Sweden before falling short of the knockout stage. Much the same team then progressed to the second round of the 2002 FIFA World Cup before falling to Brazil.

Qualifying for EURO finals proved beyond them for a decade until, in 2016, a new generation reached the quarter-finals in France. The nucleus of that team has taken Belgium to third place at the 2018 FIFA World Cup, to No1 in the world ranking and now to the EURO finals once more.

The mastermind has been Spaniard Roberto Martínez, only Belgium's second foreign coach since the late 1950s.

Real Madrid's Thibaut Courtois is established in goal behind a defence secured by Tottenham Hotspur stalwarts Toby Alderweireld and Jan Vertonghen. In midfield Martínez has been able to rely on the class and drive of Youri Tielemans, Axel Witsel and Kevin De Bruyne while Eden Hazard stars in a multi-pronged attack.

No wonder Lukaku & Co scored so freely on the way to the finals.

DID YOU KNOW?

The Red Devils fell as low as 66th in the FIFA world rankings back in 2009, but have since risen to claim the top spot in 2019.

GROUP B
RUSSIA

Revived Russia bring to the EURO a new generation of players eager to create achievements in a modern era to match the feats of legendary old heroes such as Lev Yashin and Igor Netto. They are building on a foundation of well over a century of football tradition.

Coach Stanislav Cherchesov's men became the third team to qualify for the finals after Belgium and Italy with a 5-0 victory over Cyprus in mid-October. Denis Cheryshev (two), Magomed Ozdoyev, Artem Dzyuba and Aleksandr Golovin scored the goals which confirmed their progress from Group I.

Russia's latest stars thus honoured their predecessors, since the former Soviet Union had been a dominant force in the early years of what was originally known as the Nations' Cup.

A team which won the Olympic Games gold medal in 1956 and reached the FIFA World Cup quarter-finals on their debut in 1958 went on to triumph in the inaugural tournament. This side contained some of Soviet football's greatest names, including captain Netto, inside forward Valentin Ivanov, and a great goalkeeper in Yashin.

They defeated Yugoslavia 2–1 in the final in Paris but this remains the only major national team triumph either the Soviet Union or Russia has ever

COACH

STANISLAV CHERCHESOV

Stanislav Cherchesov became one of the most popular men in Russia after guiding the Sbornaja to the quarter-finals of the FIFA World Cup as hosts in 2018. The 57-year-old had kept goal for Russia at the 1994 and 2002 World Cup finals on his way to winning 39 caps. His club career involved spells with Spartak Moscow, Dynamo Dresden and Tirol Innsbruck. He took up coaching in Austria after retiring and returned to Russia with Spartak in 2007. Cherchesov was appointed manager of Russia in succession to Leonid Slutsky in 2016.

LEFT TO RIGHT: (Back) Mário Fernandes, Georgi Dzhikiya, Andrei Semyonov, Guilherme Alvim Marinato, Artem Dzyuba. (Front) Aleksei Miranchuk, Roman Zobnin, Sergei Petrov, Aleksei Ionov, Magomed Ozdoyev, Yuri Zhirkov.

STAR PLAYER

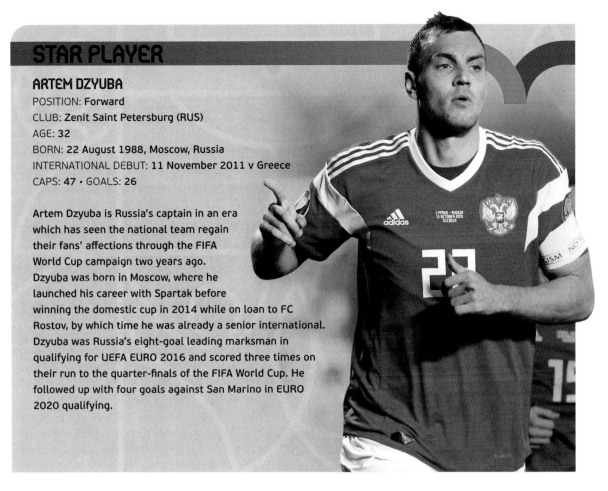

ARTEM DZYUBA

POSITION: **Forward**
CLUB: **Zenit Saint Petersburg (RUS)**
AGE: **32**
BORN: **22 August 1988, Moscow, Russia**
INTERNATIONAL DEBUT: **11 November 2011 v Greece**
CAPS: **47** · GOALS: **26**

Artem Dzyuba is Russia's captain in an era which has seen the national team regain their fans' affections through the FIFA World Cup campaign two years ago. Dzyuba was born in Moscow, where he launched his career with Spartak before winning the domestic cup in 2014 while on loan to FC Rostov, by which time he was already a senior international. Dzyuba was Russia's eight-goal leading marksman in qualifying for UEFA EURO 2016 and scored three times on their run to the quarter-finals of the FIFA World Cup. He followed up with four goals against San Marino in EURO 2020 qualifying.

celebrated. Three times they came close, finishing runners-up in 1964, 1972 and in 1988.

In between, their best FIFA World Cup performance was in reaching the semi-finals in 1966 in England. In September 1991, the Soviet Union began to fragment. The national team competed at the EURO finals the following year as the Commonwealth of Independent States.

Soon afterwards the 15 former republics began organising themselves into new and separate footballing nations with Russia picking up where the Soviet Union and CIS had left off.

Since then, Russia have reached the EURO finals six times, with their best result coming in 2008. On that occasion a team featuring goalkeeper Igor Akinfeev, central defender Sergey Ignashevich and forward Andrey

Arshavin reached the semi-finals before losing to eventual champions Spain.

Ignashevich and Akinfeev were pillars of the national team which reached the quarter-finals of the FIFA World Cup as hosts two years ago. They later retired from the national team to make way for a new younger generation inspired by their example.

Akinfeev's place in goal during the UEFA Nations League and EURO qualifying was taken over by Brazilian-born Guilherme Alvim Marinato. He took up Russian citizenship after joining Lokomotiv Moscow from Athletico Paranaense in 2007. Eight years later Guilherme became the first player naturalised from outside the former Soviet Union to play for Russia at senior international level.

In front of him, Cherchesov has looked to the experience of another

Brazilian-born stalwart in Mário Fernandes plus Fedor Kudryashov and Georgi Dzhikiya. Midfield is the realm of Aleksandr Golovin, Denis Cheryshev and veteran Yuri Zhirkov who fashion the goalscoring openings for Fedor Smolov and captain Artem Dzyuba.

Their new challenge is to improve Russia's record at the UEFA European Championship.

DID YOU KNOW?

At EURO 2020, Russia are aiming to win their first European Championship game since their 4-1 demolition of the Czech Republic at EURO 2012.

1988

MAGIC MOMENTS
Marco van Basten's perfect strike

Centre-forward Marco van Basten rounded off a triumphant Dutch campaign in Germany with a goal of appropriate magnificence. The Netherlands had begun the finals with a defeat by the Soviet Union before recovering in style. Van Basten, formerly of AFC Ajax and now with Italy's AC Milan, struck a hat-trick in a 3-1 defeat of England en route to the semi-finals. In Hamburg his late winner beat hosts West Germany and earned the Dutch a repeat against the Soviets in the final at Munich's Olympiastadion. Captain Ruud Gullit put them ahead, but the match hung in the balance before a moment of Van Basten magic. Arnold Mühren hit a long, high cross from the left and Van Basten timed his angled volley to trophy-winning perfection.

FINAL
Netherlands 2-0 Soviet Union
Olympiastadion, Munich
25 June 1988

GROUP C

Netherlands, Ukraine and Austria are accompanied by play-off winners North Macedonia. The Dutch won the EURO crown in 1988 with a victory over the Soviet Union. Ukraine and Austria have both appeared twice before in the finals, while North Macedonia are making their debut.

GROUP C
NETHERLANDS

Netherlands are back to compete at the top table of international team competition after missing out on UEFA EURO 2016 and also the FIFA World Cup in Russia in 2018. Leading them is a man who knows all about winning in coach Frank de Boer. He took up the role last September after Ronald Koeman's appointment by FC Barcelona.

The Dutch served notice of a revival of fortunes by finishing runners-up in the inaugural UEFA Nations League in 2018/19. They topped their group ahead of world champions France and former world champions Germany, then defeated England after extra time in the semi-finals. The brave run of a team built around a nucleus of experienced players and a new generation from Ajax ended only with a 1-0 defeat by hosts Portugal in the final in Porto.

In parallel, Netherlands carried their fine form into the qualifying competition for UEFA EURO 2020. They opened with a decisive 4-0 victory over Belarus then lost 3-2 at home in Amsterdam to Germany. Next time out the Dutch made amends with a 4-2 victory over the Germans away in Hamburg, with two late goals from Donyell Malen and Georginio Wijnaldum.

A goalless draw against Northern Ireland in Belfast in the penultimate

NETHERLANDS AT THE UEFA EUROPEAN CHAMPIONSHIP

1960	Did not enter
1964	Did not qualify
1968	Did not qualify
1972	Did not qualify
1976	Third place
1980	Group stage
1984	Did not qualify
1988	WINNERS
1992	Semi-finals
1996	Quarter-finals
2000	Semi-finals
2004	Semi-finals
2008	Quarter-finals
2012	Group stage
2016	Did not qualify

COACH

FRANK DE BOER

Frank de Boer was an outstanding defender for both Ajax and the Dutch national team, with whom he won 112 caps between 1990 and 2004. He won 13 major trophies with Ajax, including the UEFA Champions League and UEFA Cup, as well as the Spanish league with Barcelona. Later, he was assistant manager with the Netherlands team who reached the 2010 FIFA World Cup final, before guiding Ajax to four Dutch titles. Further spells followed with Internazionale, Crystal Palace and MLS team Atlanta United before De Boer succeeded Ronald Koeman last autumn.

LEFT TO RIGHT: (Back) Davy Pröpper, Matthijs de Ligt, Joël Veltman, Virgil van Dijk, Ryan Babel, Jasper Cillessen. (Front) Georginio Wijnaldum, Daley Blind, Memphis Depay, Frenkie de Jong Donyell Malen.

STAR PLAYER

FRENKIE DE JONG

POSITION: **Midfield**
CLUB: **Barcelona (ESP)**
AGE: **24**
BORN: **12 May 1997, Gorinchem, Netherlands**
INTERNATIONAL DEBUT: **6 September 2018 v Peru**
CAPS: **22** · GOALS: **1**

Frenkie de Jong confirmed his potential as one of European football's finest young players after joining Ajax as a teenager from Willem II in 2015. De Jong was outstanding as a defensive midfielder in Ajax's run to the semi-finals of the 2018/19 UEFA Champions League. He was subsequently hailed as the Eredivisie Player of the Season, after which he joined Spanish champions Barcelona for a €75m fee. He was also named in the 2019 FIFA FIFPro Men's World11. De Jong played more than 20 times for the Netherlands at various youth levels before making his senior international debut in September 2018, and starring in the run to the 2018/19 UEFA Nations League final, where the Dutch lost to hosts Portugal.

matchday meant that even a 5-0 victory over Estonia, with a hat-trick from Wijnaldum, was not enough to lift them above Germany. Thus the Dutch qualified for the finals as group runners-up. Liverpool midfielder Wijnaldum was the group's joint eight-goal leading scorer with Germany's Serge Gnabry.

Their talent, recent results and tradition underlines their potential at UEFA EURO 2020. The Dutch were among the continent's leading amateur teams in the early 1900s. They reached the semi-finals of four consecutive Olympic Games from 1908 to 1924 and won the bronze medal twice. A modernisation of the domestic game in the mid-1950s brought the introduction of professionalism and success both at home and abroad for Ajax of Amsterdam, Feyenoord of Rotterdam and PSV Eindhoven.

In the late 1960s and early 1970s the great coach Rinus Michels oversaw a 'total football' revolution. Johan Cruyff led record champions Ajax to three successive triumphs in the European Cup and the national team were runners-up in the FIFA World Cup in both 1974 and 1978. A new generation in the 1980s generated further European success. Ruud Gullit, Marco van Basten, Frank Rijkaard and Ronald Koeman led the national team to victory at the 1988 EURO in West Germany.

That remains Holland's only trophy. Later they were semi-finalists in the 1998 FIFA World Cup and UEFA EURO 2000, which they co-hosted with neighbours Belgium.

The present trophy-hunting generation is led by experienced defenders Virgil van Dijk and Daley

Blind, plus former Ajax graduates Matthijs de Ligt (now Juventus) and Frenkie de Jong (now Barcelona). Alongside De Jong in midfield are Wijnaldum and Donny van de Beek, while Memphis Depay leads the attack. The Lyon forward scored six goals in the qualifying competition, including doubles against both Belarus and Northern Ireland.

DID YOU KNOW?

The Dutch missed out on UEFA EURO 2016 and the 2018 FIFA World Cup. It is their longest absence from major finals since the mid-1980s... when they marked their return by winning the EURO in 1988.

GROUP C

UKRAINE

Ukraine's impressive race through the qualifying competition from an awkward group was the perfect reaction sought by Andriy Shevchenko, their coach and old goalscoring hero, to the team's group stage exit from UEFA EURO 2016 and absence from the FIFA World Cup two years later.

The draw for the qualifying competition was a challenging one. Group B featured European champions Portugal as well as Lithuania, Luxembourg and Serbia. Not only that but Ukraine's opening fixture was a visit to Cristiano Ronaldo and his team-mates in Lisbon.

Ukraine's man of the match was Shakhtar Donetsk goalkeeper Andriy Pyatov. He made a string of superb saves to foil Pepe, Ronaldo and André Silva. Even better, three days later

Ukraine went clear at the top of the group by recovering from the loss of an early goal to score a 2-1 win away to Luxembourg.

Dynamo Kyiv midfielder Viktor Tsygankov equalised and Ukraine's winner was an own goal in stoppage time. Tsygankov was on target again next time out with two goals in a 5-0 victory over Serbia.

Ukraine's winning run continued with wins at home to Luxembourg then away and home against Lithuania

COACH

ANDRIY SHEVCHENKO

Andriy Shevchenko is one of the greatest figures in the history of Ukrainian football. His appointment as national team coach in the summer of 2016 followed a free-scoring playing career. Shevchenko remains Ukraine's 48-goal leading marksman while having scored more than 250 goals at club level with Dynamo Kyiv, Milan and Chelsea. His achievements were rewarded with 18 major national and international trophies as well as the Ballon d'Or from French magazine France Football in 2004. Shevchenko has also launched a political career.

LEFT TO RIGHT: (Back) Andriy Yarmolenko, Roman Yaremchuk, Serhiy Kryvtsov, Andriy Pyatov, Serhiy Sydorchuk, Ruslan Malinovskiy. (Front) Oleksandr Karavayev, Viktor Kovalenko, Viktor Tsygankov, Mykola Matviyenko, Vitaliy Mykolenko.

STAR PLAYER

ANDRIY YARMOLENKO

POSITION: Midfielder
CLUB: West Ham United (ENG)
AGE: 31
BORN: 23 October 1989, Saint Petersburg, Russia
INTERNATIONAL DEBUT: 5 September 2009 v Andorra
CAPS: 94 · GOALS: 38

Andriy Yarmolenko brings to Ukraine's attack a versatility derived from his speed and skill on either wing and his height which makes him a threat at set pieces. In 2009 he marked his Ukraine debut with a goal in a 5-0 victory over Andorra in a FIFA World Cup qualifying tie and he went in to play in all their matches at UEFA EURO 2016. Yarmolenko was born in Russia in Leningrad, now Saint Petersburg, but the family soon moved back to their native Ukraine. As a teenager he played locally in the northern city of Chernihiv before joining Dynamo Kyiv in 2007. Yarmolenko scored 99 league goals ahead of one year in Germany with Borussia Dortmund then a move to West Ham United.

before a 2-1 defeat of Portugal in Kyiv sent Ukraine to the finals. First half goals from Roman Yaremchuk and Andriy Yarmolenko sealed the points and a place in the finals with one game to spare.

Ukraine's football pedigree was clear back in the Soviet Union era. In the 1970s and much of the 1980s the stars of Dynamo Kyiv provided a foundation for the Soviet national team while the club won the UEFA Cup Winners' Cup twice. Players such Anatoliy Byshovets then Oleg Blokhin, Viktor Kolotov and Volodymyr Onyshchenko were admired across Europe for their skill and style.

Considering the strengths of not only Dynamo Kiev but also Shakhtar Donetsk it was a surprise that Ukraine's national team took time to 'take off' after independence in the early 1990s following the fragmentation of the Soviet Union.

Not until 2006 did they qualify for the finals of the FIFA World Cup, reaching the quarter-finals in Germany. They were then absent from the major finals tournaments until UEFA EURO 2012 when they were co-hosts with Poland. Ukraine, to the disappointment of their enthusiastic home fans, were edged out of quarter-finals qualification by England and France. Group stage elimination was their fate also in France, four years later.

Shevchenko duly took over as national coach in 2016 on a two-year contract which was extended after Ukraine failed to reach the FIFA World Cup finals. That demonstration of faith was rewarded with the decisive qualification for UEFA EURO 2020.

Key men for Shevchenko included captain Pyatov in goal, Oleksandr Karavayev and Mykola Matviyenko in defence, Yarmolenko and the promising newcomer Tsygankov in midfield plus Yaremchuk and the flying winger Yevhen Konoplyanka, three times Ukraine's Footballer of the Year, in attack.

DID YOU KNOW?

This is the first time Ukraine have qualified for a EURO directly; they made it as co-hosts in 2012, and beat Slovenia in the play-offs to reach the 2016 event.

GROUP C

AUSTRIA

Austria are one of European football's great traditional nations who have lately re-established their presence at the top table. They were EURO co-hosts in 2008 with Switzerland and then qualified in their own right for the first time in France. This time they earned the right to return to the finals by finishing runners-up to Poland in qualifying Group G.

AUSTRIA AT THE UEFA EUROPEAN CHAMPIONSHIP

1960	Did not qualify
1964	Did not qualify
1968	Did not qualify
1972	Did not qualify
1976	Did not qualify
1980	Did not qualify
1984	Did not qualify
1988	Did not qualify
1992	Did not qualify
1996	Did not qualify
2000	Did not qualify
2004	Did not qualify
2008	Group stage
2012	Did not qualify
2016	Group stage

Vienna was the focal point of continental European football in the first half of the last century. In 1902 Austria beat Hungary 5-0 at the Praterstadion in what remains the world's second oldest regular international fixture after England v Scotland.

The inter-war period was Austria's most successful era, when the Wunderteam – led by Matthias Sindelar – swept all before them. In 30 matches from 1931 to 1934, Austria scored 101 goals, and the 1934 World Cup seemed to be at their mercy. But defeat in the semi-final by hosts Italy ended their dreams.

A new side came together in the 1950s, led by Ernst Ocwirk and Gerhard Hanappi, but after reaching the 1954 FIFA World Cup finals a decline set in which was underlined in 1990 by a 1-0

COACH

FRANCO FODA

Franco Foda is a former West German international who won two caps in the 1980s while playing his club football in the Bundesliga with Kaiserslautern. Foda, born 23 April 1966, also played in Switzerland with Basel and Austria with Sturm Graz before turning to coaching. He had three spells in charge of Sturm Graz, as well as a season back with Kaiserslautern, before being appointed by Austria in January 2018. Foda succeeded Marcel Koller, whose seven years in charge included leading Austria to UEFA EURO 2016.

LEFT TO RIGHT: (Back) Heinz Lindner, Martin Hinteregger, Maximilian Wöber, Peter Žulj, Xaver Schlager, Marko Arnautović. (Front) Aleksandar Dragović, Andreas Ulmer, Marcel Sabitzer, Valentino Lazaro, Julian Baumgartlinger.

STAR PLAYER

DAVID ALABA

POSITION: **Full-back or midfield**
CLUB: **FC Bayern Munich (GER)**
AGE: **29**
BORN: **24 June 1992, Vienna, Austria**
INTERNATIONAL DEBUT: **14 October 2009 v France**
CAPS: **75** · GOALS: **14**

David Alaba has had an explosive impact on the Austrian national team since becoming the country's youngest ever international when he made his debut against France aged just 17. His versatility earned him appearances on the wing, at left-back and in midfield, first in his home city of Vienna as a youth player with FK Austria and, since 2008, in Germany with Bayern Munich. Alaba played for Austria at Under-17, Under-19 and Under-21 level before being promoted to the seniors. He has been voted Austria's footballer of the year on six occasions and has won nine German Bundesliga titles and the UEFA Champions League twice, in 2013 and 2020, with Bayern. He was a key member of the national team at UEFA EURO 2016, burnishing his reputation as creative midfield anchor and penalty specialist.

defeat by the Faroe Islands, who were playing their first ever competitive match in EURO qualifying.

The road back to international respectability has been a difficult one. Austria made their debut in the European finals as co-hosts in 2008 under former international Josef Hickersberger and then returned in 2016 under Marcel Koller. Each time they were eliminated in the group stage. This was also the furthest Austria progressed on their last appearance at the finals of the FIFA World Cup in 1998.

Austria's inability to qualify for the FIFA World Cup in 2018 was followed by the appointment of Foda. The qualifying competition for UEFA EURO 2020 saw Austria drawn in Group G with Israel, Latvia, North Macedonia, Poland and Slovenia.

They opened with the disappointments of a 1-0 home defeat by eventual group winners Poland and a 4-2 loss in Israel. At this point, Austria's prospects of reaching the finals appeared slim, but successive victories over Slovenia, North Macedonia and Latvia, in which they scored a total of 11 goals and conceded only one, pulled them back on track. A solid defensive display earned a goalless draw away to Poland behind whom they ultimately qualified with a game to spare.

Austria's leading marksman with six goals was forward Marko Arnautović, who had left European club football midway through the campaign in transferring from England's West Ham United to Shanghai SIPG in China. Arnautović, who made his senior debut in 2008, has scored 26 times

for Austria in nearly 90 appearances. He is eighth in the ranking of Austria's all-time leading marksmen.

Staunch supporters of Arnautović on the road to the finals have included defenders Aleksandar Dragović and Martin Hinteregger, midfielders David Alaba, Stefan Ilsanker, and captain Julian Baumgartlinger, plus forward Marcel Sabitzer.

DID YOU KNOW?

It is nearly three decades since Austria's last victory at a major finals, when they defeated the United States 2-1 at the 1990 World Cup.

NORTH MACEDONIA

North Macedonia will be appearing in the finals of a major tournament for the first time when they kick off their UEFA EURO 2020 campaign against Austria on 13 June. Veteran captain and record appearance-holder Goran Pandev was the man who sparked the young nation's proudest sporting moment thus far, with a decisive goal in the play-off final against Georgia.

The south-east European state, with its population of just under 3 million, is landlocked between Albania to the west, Kosovo and Serbia to the north, Bulgaria to the east and Greece to the south. Independence was achieved in 1991 amid the fragmentation of the former Yugoslavia. Known initially as the Former Yugoslav Republic of Macedonia (FYROM), the current title of Republic of North Macedonia was adopted in February 2019.

This diplomatic amendment occurred just in time for the UEFA EURO 2020 qualifying competition, which North Macedonia opened with a 3-1 win over Latvia. Ezgjan Alioski claimed the honour of the first competitive goal under the new nomenclature.

North Macedonia had been drawn in a challenging Group G that also featured Poland, Austria, Slovenia and Israel, as well as Latvia. Ultimately Poland and Austria finished in the top two places to secure direct entry into the finals, with North Macedonia finishing third.

NORTH MACEDONIA AT THE UEFA EUROPEAN CHAMPIONSHIP

1960	Did not compete
1964	Did not compete
1968	Did not compete
1972	Did not compete
1976	Did not compete
1980	Did not compete
1984	Did not compete
1988	Did not compete
1992	Did not compete
1996	Did not qualify
2000	Did not qualify
2004	Did not qualify
2008	Did not qualify
2012	Did not qualify
2016	Did not qualify

COACH

IGOR ANGELOVSKI

Igor Angelovski is now enjoying his fifth year in charge of the North Macedonia national team. Angelovski was born on 2 June 1976 in Skopje, then in the former Yugoslavia. He played his club football for several local clubs and also for two years with NK Celje in Slovenia. After retiring, he launched his senior coaching career with FK Rabotnički, whom he led to North Macedonian league and cup success in 2014. The following year he was appointed as national coach in succession to Ljubinko Drulović.

LEFT TO RIGHT: (Back) Arijan Ademi, Elif Elmas, Darko Velkovski, Visar Musliu, Stole Dimitrievski, Goran Pandev. (Front) Ilija Nestorovski, Egzon Bejtulai, Ezgjan Alioski, Boban Nikolov, Stefan Ristovski.

STAR PLAYER

GORAN PANDEV

POSITION: **Striker**
CLUB: **Genoa (ITA)**
AGE: **37**
BORN: **27 July 1983, Strumica, N Macedonia**
INTERNATIONAL DEBUT: **6 June 2001 v Turkey**
CAPS: **114** • GOALS: **36**

Goran Pandev is North Macedonia's captain, inspiration and record marksman. He scored the decisive goal that secured a 1-0 play-off victory over Georgia in Tbilisi to send his team to the finals. Pandev has played almost all his senior career in Italy with Internazionale, Lazio, Napoli and Genoa, apart from a brief stint in Turkey with Galatasaray. His club honours include winner's medals in the UEFA Champions League, FIFA Cub World Cup, Serie A, Coppa Italia and Supercoppa Italiana. He has also been hailed as his nation's footballer of the year on four occasions. Pandev played his 100th international against Latvia in March 2019 and subsequently auctioned his shirt to raise funds for a hospital fighting the coronavirus pandemic.

They had followed up the opening victory over Latvia with a 1-1 draw in Slovenia before home defeats by Poland and Austria. Later came two crucial victories by 2-1 at home to Slovenia, with a double from midfielder Elif Elmas, then a 1-0 win at home to Israel on the final matchday.

That latter victory, secured by a goal in first-half stoppage time from Boban Nikolov, meant North Macedonia finished level with Slovenia on 14 points. A superior head-to-head record gave North Macedonia the advantage of third place, leaving Slovenia fourth.

A further qualifying opportunity was provided through results in the 2018-19 UEFA Nations League. North Macedonia finished five points clear of Armenia at the top of Group D4, which also featured Gibraltar and Liechtenstein. They were thus not only promoted but went forward to the UEFA EURO 2020 play-off semi-finals. Coach Igor Angelovski's men won 2-1 at home to Kosovo thanks to an own goal and a second strike from Darko Velkovski. The final away to Georgia in Tbilisi ended with Pandev emerging as the visitors' match-winning hero.

North Macedonia, however, are far from a one-man team. Goalkeeper Stole Dimitrievski, born on Christmas Day, 1993, was one of the other heroes of Tbilisi. He has been playing his football in Spain ever since he was 19 after beginning his career under Angelovski at Rabotnički.

Helping protect Dimitrievski and his goal is defender Stefan Ristovski from Sporting Club of Portugal, who has played more than 60 times for his country. In midfield, Elmas from Napoli and Leeds United's Alioski have demonstrated an ability to chip in with important goals, as has Nikolov from Hungary's Fehérvár.

The main attacking responsibility has been shouldered, for the past 18 years, by Pandev, but he is far from alone. Supporting experience has been provided by another veteran in Ivan Trichkovski from AEK Larnaca, as well as Mallorca's Aleksandar Trajkovski and Udinese's Ilija Nestorovski.

DID YOU KNOW?

North Macedonia's squad is among the most widely scattered at UEFA EURO 2020, with players representing clubs in Armenia, Belgium, Croatia, England, Estonia, Georgia, Greece, Italy, Kosovo, Portugal, Serbia and Spain.

MAGIC MOMENTS
Denmark's amazing journey

Danish dynamite proved explosive in Sweden in 1992, yet Richard Møller Nielsen's team had not qualified originally for the finals. The Danes finished runners-up in their group to Yugoslavia, who were then excluded from the finals over security concerns. Møller Nielsen had to recall some of his players from their holidays. They made a slow start, drawing with England and losing to Sweden. A 2-1 defeat of France edged them into the semi-finals, where the reflexes of goalkeeper Peter Schmeichel earned a shootout victory over the Netherlands. Denmark were outsiders yet again in the final against Germany, but goals early and late from John Jensen and Kim Vilfort crowned one of the most surprising European champions ever.

SEMI-FINAL
Denmark 2-2 (aet, pens) Netherlands
Ullevi, Gothenburg
22 June 1992

GROUP D

England, twice semi-finalists, and play-off qualifiers Scotland will reprise the world's oldest national team rivalry. The Czech Republic were champions, as the former Czechoslovakia, in 1976 and then runners-up in 1996, while Croatia have progressed twice to the quarter-finals.

GROUP D
ENGLAND

England have been going from strength to strength since former international defender Gareth Southgate took over as manager soon after the round of 16 exit from UEFA EURO 2016 in France. A team built around a bright new generation of players reached the semi-finals of both the FIFA World Cup in 2018 and then the UEFA Nations League in 2019.

The England upsurge was maintained in the manner of their qualification for the finals, which saw captain Harry Kane and his team-mates win seven of their games, scoring 37 and conceding a mere six.

The worldwide popularity of the Premier League, thus far, has been out of proportion to the national team's tradition and achievements. England contested the very first international match against Scotland in Glasgow in 1872. Yet England have won the FIFA World Cup only once, in 1966, and have never yet reached even the final of the UEFA European Championship. The nearest the Three Lions came to success was finishing third in 1968 in Italy, and then reaching the semi-finals as hosts in 1996.

A modern turning point was England's exit from the FIFA World Cup in 2014 after only two games in the group stage. Brazil saw the

COACH

GARETH SOUTHGATE

Gareth Southgate was a central defender and defensive midfielder who played 57 times for England between 1995 and 2004, including the finals of the FIFA World Cup in 1998 and UEFA European Championship in 1996 and 2000. Southgate managed Middlesbrough from 2006 until 2009 before joining the Football Association. He coached the England Under-21s from 2013 to 2016, bringing through many of his current players, before becoming senior manager. He is the third man, after Sir Alf Ramsey and Sir Bobby Robson, to lead England to a World Cup semi-final.

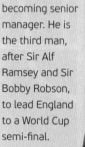

LEFT TO RIGHT: (Back) Kyle Walker, Michael Keane, Eric Dier, Jordan Pickford, Harry Maguire, Jordan Henderson, Dele Alli. (Front) Ben Chilwell, Harry Kane, Raheem Sterling, Jadon Sancho.

STAR PLAYER

RAHEEM STERLING

POSITION: **Forward**
CLUB: **Manchester City (ENG)**
AGE: **26**
BORN: **8 December 1994, Kingston, Jamaica**
INTERNATIONAL DEBUT: **14 November 2012 v Sweden**
CAPS: **58 • GOALS: 13**

Raheem Sterling has developed into one of the most dangerous forwards in European football in a club career that has taken him from Queens Park Rangers to Liverpool and then Manchester City, for a then English player record of £49m in 2015. Initially a winger, Jamaican-born Sterling graduated into an all-areas striker. He scored 35 goals in City's Premier League title triumphs in 2018 and 2019. In the latter season he was also hailed as footballer of the year by both his fellow players and by the Football Writers' Association. With England, Sterling progressed via the Under-16, Under-17, Under-19 and Under-21 levels to become a firm fixture in the senior squads at the 2014 and 2018 FIFA World Cups, and UEFA EURO 2016.

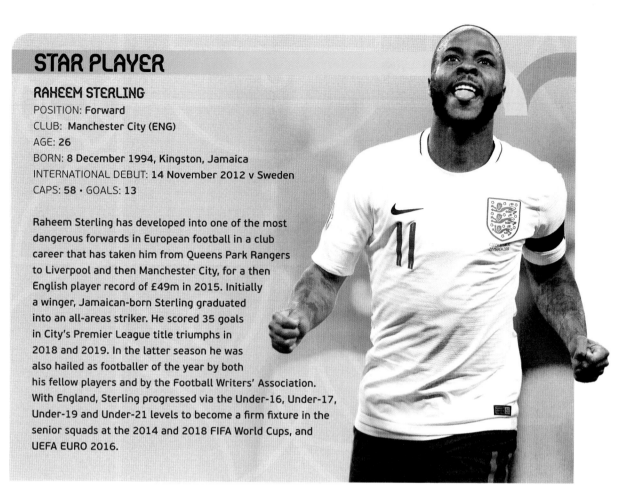

international farewells of long-serving stalwarts such as midfielders Steven Gerrard and Frank Lampard, and it was a team in transition under Roy Hodgson, which fell to Iceland in the knockout stage of UEFA EURO 2016.

Key players under Southgate over the past two years have included the Everton goalkeeper Jordan Pickford, Manchester United central defender Harry Maguire, Liverpool captain Jordan Henderson in midfield, plus Kane and Raheem Sterling in attack. Kane was the leading marksman in the entire qualifying competition with 12 goals.

The journey to the 2020 finals saw this nucleus joined by emerging young talents in Chelsea left-back Ben Chilwell, midfielders Harry Winks and Declan Rice from London rivals Tottenham and West Ham, plus wingers Jadon Sancho and Callum Hudson-Odoi from Borussia Dortmund and Chelsea respectively.

England were drawn in qualifying Group A along with an eastern European quartet in Bulgaria, the Czech Republic, Kosovo and Montenegro. They signalled their power and intent by opening the campaign in March 2019 with a 5-0 victory over the Czech Republic in front an 82,575 attendance at Wembley. Sterling claimed a hat-trick and Kane two in a sequence which saw him score at least once in all eight group games.

The goals continued to flow over the next three matches: five in Montenegro, four at home to Bulgaria then a further five against Kosovo in an entertaining 5-3 victory staged not at Wembley, but in Southampton. England suffered a lone defeat in the Czech Republic, but reacted in style by winning 6-0 in Bulgaria, scoring seven more against Montenegro and finally four against Kosovo.

England had never scored so freely in a qualifying campaign, while Kane's goal in Pristina lifted him to a record-equalling 12 in a calendar year for his country, matching the feats of George Hilson in 1908 and Dixie Dean in 1927.

DID YOU KNOW?

The Three Lions were 43 successive European Championship and World Cup qualifiers without defeat until their loss to the Czech Republic in October 2019.

GROUP D

CROATIA

Croatia have commanded a high profile in international football ever since the country became independent out of the former Yugoslavia in the early 1990s. They reached the quarter-finals in their debut tournament at EURO '96 and Davor Šuker, then their leading scorer, had become president of the Croatian Football Federation by the time they reached the 2018 FIFA World Cup final in Russia.

Only twice have Croatia's famous chequered red and white shirts not lit up the finals of a major international tournament. They missed out on the World Cup finals only in 2010 and EURO in 2000.

The Croatia team who reached the EURO quarter-finals in 1996 went on to finish third at the FIFA World Cup in France two years later. Key players included not only Šuker but playmakers Zvonimir

Boban and Robert Prosinečki, all of them previously FIFA World Youth Championship winners with Yugoslavia in 1987. Šuker scored six goals in France to win the Golden Boot as the tournament's leading scorer.

Since then, Croatia have been regular contenders in both the FIFA World Cup and at EURO, at which they reached the quarter-finals in Austria and Switzerland

CROATIA AT THE UEFA EUROPEAN CHAMPIONSHIP

1960	Did not compete
1964	Did not compete
1968	Did not compete
1972	Did not compete
1976	Did not compete
1980	Did not compete
1984	Did not compete
1988	Did not compete
1992	Did not compete
1996	Quarter-finals
2000	Did not qualify
2004	Group stage
2008	Quarter-finals
2012	Group stage
2016	Round of 16

COACH

ZLATKO DALIĆ

Zlatko Dalić, 54, succeeded Ante Čačić as coach of Croatia ahead of the 2018 FIFA World Cup finals in which they finished runners-up after losing 4-2 to France. Previously Dalić had led the Under-21s between 2006 and 2011. At club level he coached Varteks, Rijeka, Slaven Belupo and Albania's Dinamo Tirana before heading for the Middle East. Here he coached clubs in Saudi Arabia, then Al Ain in the United Arab Emirates. They won the UAE Pro League and UAE Super Cup in 2015 and were runners-up in the 2016 AFC Champions League.

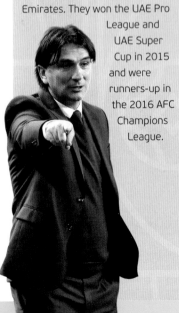

LEFT TO RIGHT: (Front) Borna Barišić, Marcelo Brozović, Tin Jedvaj, Nikola Vlašić, Luka Modrić. (Back) Duje Ćaleta-Car, Bruno Petković, Dino Perić, Ante Rebić, Dominik Livaković, Ivan Perišić.

STAR PLAYER

IVAN PERIŠIĆ

POSITION: **Forward**
CLUB: **Internazionale (ITA)**
AGE: **32**
BORN: **2 February 1989, Split, Croatia**
INTERNATIONAL DEBUT: **26 March 2011 v Georgia**
CAPS: **96 · GOALS: 26**

Ivan Perišić commands a particular place in Croatia football history as their first player to score a goal in a FIFA World Cup final. That was in 2018, when Perišić's strike brought Croatia briefly back on terms at 1-1 in the eventual 4-2 defeat by France. Previously he was a goal-scoring official man of the match in the 2-1 semi-final victory over England. The hard-working winger had played in the 2014 FIFA World Cup as well as the finals of UEFA EURO 2012 and 2016. Perišić, who was born in Split in the former Yugoslavia, has played all his senior career in France, Belgium, Germany and currently Italy with Internazionale. Last season he was on loan to Bayern Munich, whom he helped win the UEFA Champions League after recovering from an ankle fracture.

in 2008. On the latter occasion they were desperately unlucky not to reach the last four after losing a dramatic clash to Turkey only on penalties after extra time in Vienna. In France five years ago they reached the round of 16 before losing after extra time to eventual champions Portugal.

Croatia were one of the most efficient of the qualifying nations for UEFA EURO 2020. They topped Group E though none of the other group winners scored fewer than the 17-goal tally they shared with Ukraine from Group B.

There was rarely any doubt that they would reach the finals after they had recovered from the slip of a second matchday setback in Hungary. The 2-1 defeat was Croatia's only loss in their eight games and they

were certain of qualification with a game to spare. Croatia conceded seven goals and finished with a goal difference of +10.

Dinamo Zagreb forward Bruno Petković was the group's four-goal top scorer. Ivan Perišić and Nikola Vlašić each scored three. The three men scored Croatia's goals in the 3-1 win over Slovakia with which they wrapped up their group campaign. Croatia's captain and playmaker Luka Modrić contributed two goals along with some inspirational performances in midfield.

Further established stars on whom coach Zlatko Dalić could rely included central defenders Domagoj Vida from Turkey's Beşiktaş and Dejan Lovren from Zenit St Petersburg. The latter had been at the heart of the defence of the Liverpool team who won the

UEFA Champions League in 2019.

In midfield, support for the experienced partnership of Modrić and Ivan Rakitić was provided by the hard-working Milan Badelj, Marcelo Brozović and Mateo Kovačić. The attack saw the emergence of Petković provide additional firepower alongside the veteran Perišić.

DID YOU KNOW?

Croatia climbed an astonishing 122 places in the FIFA rankings from 125th to third during their successful run between 1994 and 1999.

GROUP D
SCOTLAND

Scotland are back at a major finals for the first time in 23 years. Their last appearance in the international limelight was at the FIFA World Cup in 1998. Previously the Scots and their Tartan Army of fans had shared in two campaigns at the UEFA European Championship finals. They did not progress beyond the group stage, however, either in Sweden in 1992 or in England in 1996.

Absence from a place among the headline-makers thus far this century has been a painful blow to the pride of Scottish fans, players and officials. Scotland, after all, contested the historic first-ever international match when they drew 0-0 with England in Partick, Glasgow, on 30 November 1872.

Later it was Scots who devised the passing game and who sent the first professionals south across the border into England. For much of the 20th century most English league clubs featured a nucleus of outstanding Scots.

'Old Firm' rivals Celtic and Rangers were redoubtable opponents in the early years of the continental club competitions and Celtic, in 1967, were the first British club to win the European Champion Clubs' Cup. Rangers won the Cup Winners' Cup in 1972.

The financial and competitive map of European football has

COACH

STEVE CLARKE

Steve Clarke has been manager of Scotland since May 2019 when he succeeded Alex McLeish. Clarke, born on 29 August 1963, began his playing career with St Mirren before spending 11 years and making more than 400 appearances in defence for Chelsea in England. He won the UEFA Cup Winners' Cup, the League Cup and FA Cup and played six times for Scotland. His management career featured spells with West Bromwich Albion, Reading, Aston Villa and Kilmarnock back in Scotland, before his national team appointment.

LEFT TO RIGHT: (Back) Andrew Robertson, Stephen O'Donnell, Ryan Jack, Declan Gallagher, Lyndon Dykes, David Marshall. (Front) Scott McTominay, Callum McGregor, John McGinn, Kieran Tierney, Ryan Christie.

STAR PLAYER

DAVID MARSHALL

POSITION: **Goalkeeper**
CLUB: **Derby County (ENG)**
AGE: **36**
BORN: **5 March 1985, Glasgow, Scotland**
INTERNATIONAL DEBUT: **18 August 2004 v Hungary**
CAPS: **41** · GOALS: **0**

David Marshall's goalkeeping reflexes and saves proved decisive in both the play-off shootout victories over Israel and Serbia, which took Scotland to the UEFA EURO 2020 finals. He boasts the longest international career span of any of Scotland's 1,200-plus players, having won his first cap 17 years ago in 2004. Marshall rose through the Celtic youth system and won league, league cup and Scottish cup medals before transferring to English football in 2007 with Norwich City. Later he helped Welsh club Cardiff City win promotion to the English Premier League in 2013 and became team captain. Subsequent moves took him to Hull City, Wigan Athletic and then to Derby County in the English second tier last year.

been redrawn since then. Scotland have suffered a number of disappointments in EURO qualifying, with play-off defeats by England in 1999 and Netherlands in 2003 being the nearest misses.

They have ended more than two decades out in the cold courtesy of the extra route provided by the 2018-19 UEFA Nations League. The mainstream UEFA EURO 2020 qualifying competition saw Scotland finish a distant third in Group I, 15 points behind Belgium and nine adrift of second-placed Russia. Their last hope of qualifying directly vanished all the way back in October 2019 after a 4-0 defeat in Russia with three matches still to play.

Enter the lifeline of the Nations League, which kept qualification a possibility. They had topped Group C1 to earn a play-off semi-final against Israel. A goalless extra-time draw propelled Scotland into the

first shootout in their history. David Marshall saved Eran Zahavi's opening effort for Israel and Kenny McLean despatched the decisive kick to earn a final trip to face Serbia in Belgrade. This time they won another shootout 4-2 after a 1-1 draw, with Marshall decisively defying Aleksandar Mitrović.

Manager Steve Clarke was praised widely for turning his team around after defeats in four of his first five matches in charge. Between the defeat in Russia and the success in Belgrade, Scotland went nine games without defeat. Clarke was rewarded in full for recalling Marshall in goal and putting his faith in Motherwell central defender Declan Gallagher and Australia-born striker Lyndon Dykes.

Clarke possesses international-class left wing-backs in captain Andrew Robertson from Liverpool and Arsenal's Kieran Tierney, plus well-balanced midfielders

in Manchester United's Scott McTominay and Aston Villa's John McGinn.

Scotland have also regained confidence and pride. As Clarke said in Belgrade: "Sometimes the fear of losing can overcome the anticipation of winning, so I told them before the game: 'Make sure you anticipate winning this game, don't play with fear.' And they didn't play with fear, so we're going away as winners and that's massive."

DID YOU KNOW?

Scotland missed out on a place at the finals of UEFA EURO 2000 after manager Craig Brown's team lost a play-off to historic rivals and neighbours England.

CZECH REPUBLIC

Czech football has been a central force in the European game for the past century, whatever the politically drawn borders. Jaroslav Šilhavý brings to the finals of UEFA EURO 2016 a team representing a nation who can look back with optimism born of the pride from victory back in 1976, and most recently a presence at the finals for all the past six tournaments.

CZECH REPUBLIC AT THE UEFA EUROPEAN CHAMPIONSHIP*

1960	Third place
1964	Did not qualify
1968	Did not qualify
1972	Did not qualify
1976	WINNERS
1980	Third place
1984	Did not qualify
1988	Did not qualify
1992	Did not qualify
1996	Runners-up
2000	Group stage
2004	Semi-finals
2008	Group stage
2012	Quarter-finals
2016	Group stage

*1960-92 as Czechoslovakia

The Czechs were drawn in Group A of the qualifying tournament with Bulgaria, England, Kosovo and Montenegro. For most of the campaign they squabbled over the runners-up spot in the group with Kosovo and, notably, ended as the only team who inflicted a defeat on eventual pool winners England, by 2-1 in Prague last October. They reached the finals as group runners-up, six points behind England.

Coach Jaroslav Šilhavý and his men started disappointingly, with a 5-0 away defeat by England at Wembley. They recovered their equilibrium with victories at home to Bulgaria and Montenegro before losing 2-1 in Kosovo, despite having taken an early lead through Patrik Schick. Victories over Montenegro and England followed before the decisive qualifying tie against Kosovo back in Plzeň.

COACH

JAROSLAV ŠILHAVÝ

Jaroslav Šilhavý succeeded Karel Jarolím in 2018 in time for the UEFA Nations League and then EURO qualifying. As a player, he made a record 465 appearances in the Czech league as a defender over two decades with Škoda Plzeň, RH Cheb, Slavia Praha, Petra Drnovice and Viktoria Plzeň. After retiring in 1999 he graduated into coaching with SK Kladno, Viktoria Plzen, Dynamo České Budějovice, Slovan Liberec, Baumit Jablonec, Dukla and Slavia Praha. He won the league with Liberec in 2012 and Slavia in 2017.

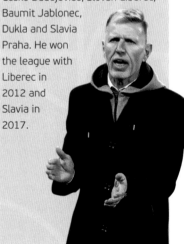

LEFT TO RIGHT: (Front) Vladimír Coufal, Vladimír Darida, Lukáš Masopust, Jan Bořil, Jakub Jankto. (Back) Tomáš Vaclík, Jakub Brabec, Alex Král, Tomáš Souček, Ondřej Čelůstka, Michael Krmenčík.

STAR PLAYER

VLADIMÍR DARIDA

POSITION: Midfield
CLUB: Hertha Berlin (GER)
AGE: 30
BORN: 8 August 1990, Plzeň, Czech Republic
INTERNATIONAL DEBUT: 21 June 2012 v Portugal
CAPS: 67 • GOALS: 8

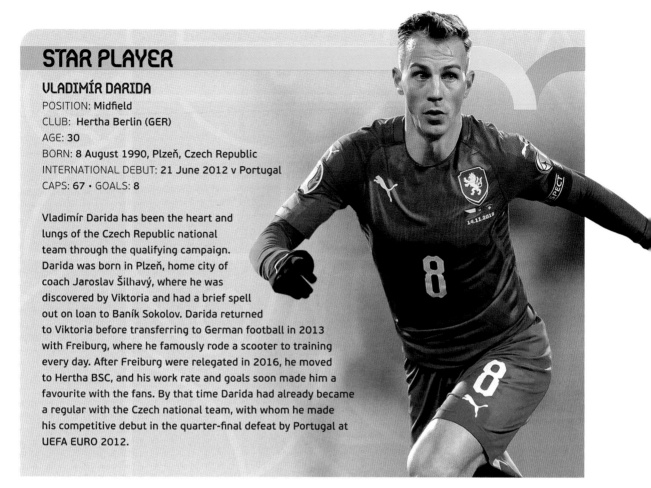

Vladimír Darida has been the heart and lungs of the Czech Republic national team through the qualifying campaign. Darida was born in Plzeň, home city of coach Jaroslav Šilhavý, where he was discovered by Viktoria and had a brief spell out on loan to Baník Sokolov. Darida returned to Viktoria before transferring to German football in 2013 with Freiburg, where he famously rode a scooter to training every day. After Freiburg were relegated in 2016, he moved to Hertha BSC, and his work rate and goals soon made him a favourite with the fans. By that time Darida had already became a regular with the Czech national team, with whom he made his competitive debut in the quarter-final defeat by Portugal at UEFA EURO 2012.

A crisis loomed when Atdhe Nuhiu put Kosovo ahead soon after half-time, but the Czechs recovered dramatically with goals from Alex Král and Ondřej Čelůstka. That lifted them four points clear of Kosovo and rendered their last game defeat against Bulgaria merely academic. Schick from RB Leipzig, on loan from Roma, was their leading scorer with four goals.

Tomáš Vaclík, from Spain's Sevilla, is the Czechs' most experienced goalkeeper in a role that has been commanded by outstanding personalities, from František Plánička in the 1930s to most recently Petr Čech. Pavel Kadeřábek, Marek Suchý and Theodor Gebre Selassie offer experience in defence.

Vladimír Darida has proved a peripatetic playmaker in midfielder alongside Bořek Dočkal and Tomáš Souček, making the chances for Schick and Matěj Vydra.

The history of Czech football traces back more than a century before Czechoslovakia had even been founded. The First World War led to the creation of a new national identity and the Czechs were among Europe's leading football nations throughout the inter-war years. Sparta and Slavia dominated the Mitropa Cup – forerunner of the present European club tournaments – and the national team were runners-up in the 1934 FIFA World Cup.

After the Second World War, the army club Dukla, led by the great midfielder Josef Masopust, provided the foundation for a national team that were runners-up to Brazil at the FIFA World Cup in 1962. Czechoslovakia were also among the early powers in the European Championship, winning a thrilling final in 1976 and finishing third in 1980.

A quarter-final appearance at the 1990 FIFA World Cup in Italy proved an international swansong before the parting of the Czech Republic and Slovakia. Runners-up spot at EURO '96 in England and a semi-final appearance in 2004 proved that the Czechs remained a power in the game.

DID YOU KNOW?

Czech Republic are ever-present at the UEFA European Championship as an independent nation, reaching seven successive finals tournaments including EURO 2020.

1996

MAGIC MOMENTS
Bierhoff's golden goal

Oliver Bierhoff made history with the first golden goal in a major competition when Germany won the EURO crown for the third time in England in 1996. Bierhoff, then with Italian club Udinese, was a 28-year-old late-comer to international football when he was named in trainer Berti Vogts's squad. Germany were 1-0 down in the final at Wembley with 21 minutes remaining when he stepped off the substitutes' bench in place of Mehmet Scholl. With almost his first touch Bierhoff equalised by heading home a free-kick from Christian Ziege. That took the final into extra time where Bierhoff struck again, in the 95th minute. The rules applying to the experimental golden goal rule meant that the match ended immediately, with Germany the champions and Bierhoff their history-creating hero.

FINAL
Czech Republic 1-2 (aet) Germany
Wembley Stadium, London
30 June 1996

1996

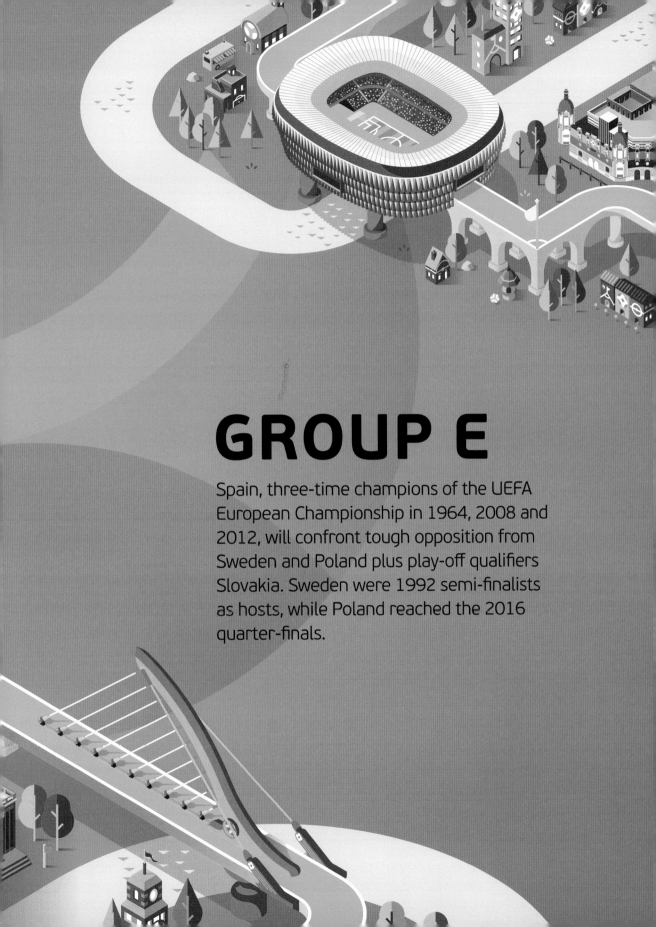

GROUP E

Spain, three-time champions of the UEFA European Championship in 1964, 2008 and 2012, will confront tough opposition from Sweden and Poland plus play-off qualifiers Slovakia. Sweden were 1992 semi-finalists as hosts, while Poland reached the 2016 quarter-finals.

GROUP E
SPAIN

Spain are one of the most successful nations in the history of the UEFA European Championship. They have celebrated title triumphs on three occasions, in 1964, 2008 and 2012, and finished as runners-up in 1984. Victory at Wembley in July would establish them as the unchallenged No1.

Yet at one time Spain's reputation as a world power in football was based almost exclusively on the exploits of its world-famous clubs, particularly Real Madrid and Barcelona. Then the national team embarked on a sensational run of three major tournament triumphs between 2008 and 2012 to confirm Spanish football as dominant in every sphere.

Football first gained a foothold in the late 19th century, followed by the foundation in 1913 of the Real Federación Española de Fútbol. The national team made their debut at the Olympic Games in Antwerp in 1920. They reached the quarter-finals of both the 1928 Olympics and 1934 World Cup with a team starring legendary goalkeeper Ricardo Zamora.

Madrid and Barcelona, the Clásico rivals, brought glamour and glory to the early years of European club competition in the 1950s, largely

LEFT TO RIGHT: (Back) Rodrigo, Sergio Ramos, Gerard Moreno, Raúl Albiol, Pau López, Alvaro Morata. (Front) Juan Bernat, Santi Cazorla, Jesús Navas, Pablo Sarabia, Thiago Alcântara.

SPAIN AT THE UEFA EUROPEAN CHAMPIONSHIP

1960	Withdrew
1964	WINNERS
1968	Did not qualify
1972	Did not qualify
1976	Did not qualify
1980	Group stage
1984	Runners-up
1988	Group stage
1992	Did not qualify
1996	Quarter-finals
2000	Quarter-finals
2004	Group stage
2008	WINNERS
2012	WINNERS
2016	Round of 16

COACH

LUIS ENRIQUE

Luis Enrique is another in a long line of Spanish national team coaches who had also been international players. Born in Gijón, in north-west Spain, he played for his local club, then Real Madrid and Barcelona at both inside forward and full-back. His honours include a gold medal from the 1982 Olympic Games. Luis Enrique's coaching career took him to Roma in Italy, then home with Celta and Barcelona, whom he led to UEFA Champions League success in 2015. He was appointed Spain coach in 2018 then reappointed in November 2019 after a six-month break for family reasons.

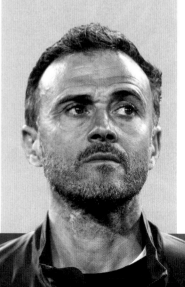

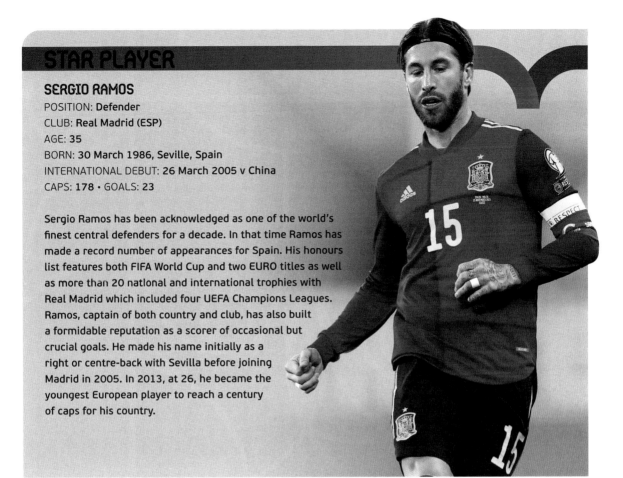

SERGIO RAMOS

POSITION: **Defender**
CLUB: **Real Madrid (ESP)**
AGE: **35**
BORN: **30 March 1986, Seville, Spain**
INTERNATIONAL DEBUT: **26 March 2005 v China**
CAPS: **178** · GOALS: **23**

Sergio Ramos has been acknowledged as one of the world's finest central defenders for a decade. In that time Ramos has made a record number of appearances for Spain. His honours list features both FIFA World Cup and two EURO titles as well as more than 20 national and international trophies with Real Madrid which included four UEFA Champions Leagues. Ramos, captain of both country and club, has also built a formidable reputation as a scorer of occasional but crucial goals. He made his name initially as a right or centre-back with Sevilla before joining Madrid in 2005. In 2013, at 26, he became the youngest European player to reach a century of caps for his country.

on the back of imported talent. Madrid boasted Argentina's Alfredo Di Stéfano and Hungarian Ferenc Puskás, while Barca had their own Hungarian trio of László Kubala, Sándor Kocsis and Zoltán Czibor.

Now new Spanish heroes emerged. Barcelona playmaker Luis Suárez and Madrid winger Amancio were key members of the Spain side which, as hosts, won their initial European crown in 1964. They defeated holders the Soviet Union 2–1 in Madrid's Estadio Bernabéu.

The national team had limited success for two decades until a revival brought quarter-finals progress at the 1986 FIFA World Cup in Mexico. Six years later Spain's youngsters won Olympic gold in Barcelona with a team including Pep Guardiola whose

coaching work would later help revitalise the national team.

Spain's seniors reached the quarter-finals of both the 1994 FIFA World Cup and EURO '96 before securing command of the world and European game in the 21st century. The tiki taka possession game revolution saw Spain beat Germany 1-0 at UEFA EURO 2008, the Netherlands by the same margin at the 2010 FIFA World Cup then Italy 4-0 at UEFA EURO 2012.

Captain Sergio Ramos, wing-backs Jordi Alba and Jesús Navas plus midfield anchor Sergio Busquets were European winners eight years ago who also helped secure a place in the 2020 finals. Ramos struck the winning goal from a penalty in the opening tie at home to Norway. Spain followed up with successive

victories over Malta, Faroe Islands (twice), Sweden and Romania.

Qualification was achieved after 1-1 draws away to Norway and Sweden though Spain needed a stoppage-time equaliser in Solna from Rodrigo to book their place at the finals with two matches to spare.

History beckons.

DID YOU KNOW?

Sergio Ramos has now overtaken Iker Casillas as Spain's record caps holder. He'll hope to extend his lead at EURO 2020.

GROUP E

SWEDEN

Sweden will be presenting a new face at UEFA EURO 2020 after the national team retirement of Zlatan Ibrahimović in 2016, who provided so much inspiration over many years. However, their traditional values of teamwork, tactical discipline and selfless running will continue to make life difficult for whoever they face at any stage of the competition.

Traditionally the Swedes have been among the most consistently formidable opponents in international football. Nowadays that consistency is built on a solid defensive foundation created by Mikael Lustig, Victor Lindelöf and captain Andreas Granqvist from Helsingborg. The latter has also played in England, the Netherlands, Italy and Russia.

Midfield is the domain of Emil Forsberg, Albin Ekdal and veteran Sebastian Larsson, who has won well over 100 caps for his country since 2008. In attack, Sweden have had to learn to live without the genius of Ibrahimović. The weight of responsibility for goals now falls squarely on the shoulders of Marcus Berg and former European Under-21 champions Robin Quaison and John Guidetti.

Sweden's greatest era in football history was in the late 1940s and 1950s. Those were the days when they boasted one of the most famous

SWEDEN AT THE UEFA EUROPEAN CHAMPIONSHIP

1960	Did not enter
1964	Did not qualify
1968	Did not qualify
1972	Did not qualify
1976	Did not qualify
1980	Did not qualify
1984	Did not qualify
1988	Did not qualify
1992	Semi-finals
1996	Did not qualify
2000	Group stage
2004	Quarter-finals
2008	Group stage
2012	Group stage
2016	Group stage

COACH

JANNE ANDERSSON

Jan Olof 'Janne' Andersson took over as national manager from Erik Hamrén after Sweden had been eliminated in the group stage of UEFA EURO 2016 in France. Previously Andersson had coached Swedish clubs Halmstad, Örgryte and Norrköping. He was voted Coach of the Year in 2004 after leading Halmstad to second place in the Swedish championship. Andersson celebrated his first league title win with Norrköping in 2015. He had spent almost all his playing career with Alets IK, with whom he was club record scorer.

LEFT TO RIGHT: (Back) Robin Olsen, Marcus Berg, Andreas Granqvist, Filip Helander, Robin Quaison, Kristoffer Olsson. (Front) Mikael Lustig, Viktor Claesson, Ludwig Augustinsson, Sebastian Larsson, Emil Forsberg

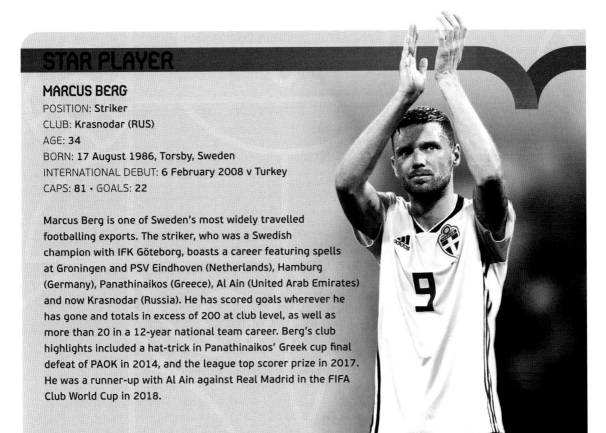

STAR PLAYER

MARCUS BERG

POSITION: Striker
CLUB: Krasnodar (RUS)
AGE: **34**
BORN: **17 August 1986, Torsby, Sweden**
INTERNATIONAL DEBUT: **6 February 2008 v Turkey**
CAPS: **81** · GOALS: **22**

Marcus Berg is one of Sweden's most widely travelled footballing exports. The striker, who was a Swedish champion with IFK Göteborg, boasts a career featuring spells at Groningen and PSV Eindhoven (Netherlands), Hamburg (Germany), Panathinaikos (Greece), Al Ain (United Arab Emirates) and now Krasnodar (Russia). He has scored goals wherever he has gone and totals in excess of 200 at club level, as well as more than 20 in a 12-year national team career. Berg's club highlights included a hat-trick in Panathinaikos' Greek cup final defeat of PAOK in 2014, and the league top scorer prize in 2017. He was a runner-up with Al Ain against Real Madrid in the FIFA Club World Cup in 2018.

forward lines in history. Gunnar Gren, Gunnar Nordahl and Nils Liedholm sparked Sweden to Olympic gold in 1948 and were promptly signed up by Milan. They enjoyed further success in Italy, where they were nicknamed the 'Gre-No-Li' trio.

The Swedes finished third in the 1950 FIFA World Cup after discovering a new star in winger Lennart 'Nacka' Skoglund. Eight years later Sweden not only hosted the World Cup but reached the final before succumbing 5-2 to a Brazilian team featuring the 17-year-old Pelé.

Sweden qualified for all three World Cup finals tournaments in the 1970s when central defender Bjorn Nordqvist tallied a then record 115 appearances. Simultaneously Sweden's clubs began to make an impact on the international stage.

Malmo reached the European Cup final in 1979 and IFK Gothenburg won the UEFA Cup twice.

Sweden's first appearance in the European Championship finals came in 1992. They were entered directly into the finals by virtue of being hosts and reached the last four before losing to Germany. They followed up by finishing third at the 1994 World Cup in the United States.

The 21st century has been less rewarding. Sweden have been ever-present at the EURO finals ever since 2000, though their best finish was reaching the quarter-finals in 2004. They also reached the quarter-finals of the FIFA World Cup in Russia in 2018.

Sweden opened their UEFA EURO 2020 qualifying campaign in Group F in positive fashion with a 2-1 victory over Romania in Solna.

However, they were held to draws twice by pursuers Norway and lost away and drew at home against group favourites Spain. Eventually a 2-0 victory over Romania in the penultimate matchday clinched the Swedes' place in the finals for an impressive sixth successive time. Quaison and the ever-reliable Berg scored the goals.

DID YOU KNOW?

In 1992, Sweden won a group ahead of England, France and eventual victors Denmark before being edged out 3-2 by Germany in the semis.

GROUP E

POLAND

The awesome attacking power of record marksman Robert Lewandowski marks out Poland as a danger to all other contenders at UEFA EURO 2020. Coach Paulo Sousa's team will be lighting up the finals for the fourth successive time with the aim of improving on their quarter-final finish five years ago.

Poland secured their ticket to the finals in mid-October with a 2-0 home victory over North Macedonia. They were forced to wait for the right to celebrate. Not until 16 minutes from the final whistle did they break through with a goal from substitute Przemysław Frankowski.

Six minutes later another replacement, Arkadiusz Milik, struck the decisive second. Poland thus reached the finals with two Group G matches in hand. They enjoyed

the right to celebrate after having overcome the earlier disappointment of finishing bottom of their UEFA Nations League group.

The national team have now existed for almost a century, the country's independence in 1921 being followed by a first international against Hungary. Poland then made their debut at the FIFA World Cup finals in 1938 when Ernest Wilimowski scored a hat-trick in a dramatic first round defeat by Brazil. That remained their last

COACH

PAULO SOUSA

Paulo Sousa was a member of the Portuguese 'golden generation' of the late 1980s and early 1990s. An outstanding midfielder, he won back-to-back UEFA Champions League titles with Juventus and Borussia Dortmund, and played 52 times for the senior national team between 1991 and 2002. Sousa launched his coaching career with the Portugal youth teams before working in eight different countries, winning major club trophies in Hungary, Israel and Switzerland. He succeeded Jerzy Brzęczek as Poland's national coach in January 2021.

LEFT TO RIGHT: (Back) Grzegorz Krychowiak, Arkadiusz Reca, Jan Bednarek, Wojciech Szczęsny, Łukasz Piszczek, Kamil Glik. (Front) Sebastian Szymański, Jacek Góralski, Kamil Grosicki, Robert Lewandowski, Piotr Zieliński.

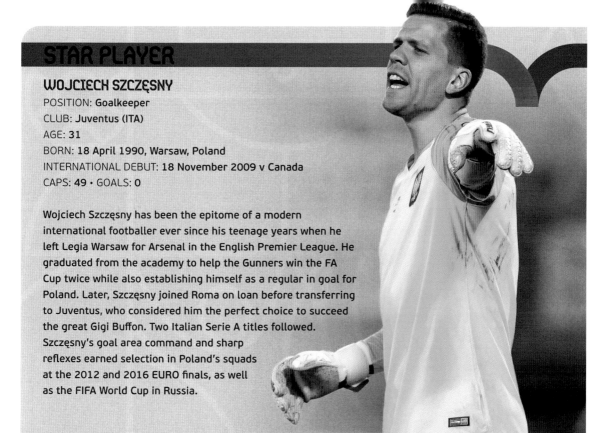

STAR PLAYER

WOJCIECH SZCZĘSNY

POSITION: Goalkeeper
CLUB: Juventus (ITA)
AGE: 31
BORN: 18 April 1990, Warsaw, Poland
INTERNATIONAL DEBUT: 18 November 2009 v Canada
CAPS: 49 · GOALS: 0

Wojciech Szczęsny has been the epitome of a modern international footballer ever since his teenage years when he left Legia Warsaw for Arsenal in the English Premier League. He graduated from the academy to help the Gunners win the FA Cup twice while also establishing himself as a regular in goal for Poland. Later, Szczęsny joined Roma on loan before transferring to Juventus, who considered him the perfect choice to succeed the great Gigi Buffon. Two Italian Serie A titles followed. Szczęsny's goal area command and sharp reflexes earned selection in Poland's squads at the 2012 and 2016 EURO finals, as well as the FIFA World Cup in Russia.

appearance at a major finals for more than three decades.

A revival of Polish football was signalled by the progress of Górnik Zabrze to the final of the UEFA Cup Winners' Cup in 1969. Three years later, Poland won the football gold medal at the Munich Olympic Games with a side starring striker Wlodzimierz Lubanski, playmaker Kazimierz Deyna and left-winger Robert Gadocha.

The successive arrival of stars such as striker Grzegorz Lato and goalkeeper Jan Tomaszewski followed later by Zbigniew Boniek saw Poland finish third at the FIFA World Cups of 1974 and 1982. Both Lato and Boniek later became presidents of the Polish Football Federation.

Despite that success on the world stage, Poland didn't play at a UEFA European Championship finals until 2008, when they were joint-hosts

with Ukraine. However, both then and four years later, they were unable to progress out of their group.

They overcame that hurdle at UEFA EURO 2016 in France. Then Poland, benefiting from the outstanding marksmanship of Germany-based centre-forward Robert Lewandowski, fell only in a penalty shootout to eventual champions Portugal in the quarter-finals.

The solid backbone of that team ensured Poland maintained momentum to reach the group stage of the 2018 FIFA World Cup in Russia and are now back to the EURO finals for a fourth successive occasion.

At the back, coach Paulo Sousa can look to goalkeeper Wojciech Szczęsny and defenders Kamil Glik, Maciej Rybus and Artur Jędrzejczyk who share more than 225 international appearances between them. Ahead of them, Kamil

Grosicki, from English Premier League club West Bromwich Albion, presents the greatest goalscoring threat from midfield with the support of Grzegorz Krychowiak.

The total of all Poland's teamwork, however, is focused on creating the goalscoring openings for Lewandowski and Arkadiusz Milik. Their success will define whether Poland can emulate their campaign in France.

DID YOU KNOW?

Paulo Sousa is only the second foreigner to manage Poland in more than half a century. Dutchman Leo Beenhakker was the last non-Polish manager to take the job, from 2006 to 2009.

GROUP E
SLOVAKIA

Slovakia are returning to UEFA EURO 2020 after making their finals debut in France five years ago, when they progressed through the group stage to the round of 16. This time around, they missed out on direct qualification but reached the finals with a dramatic extra-time victory away to Northern Ireland in Belfast in the play-offs.

Slovakia had finished third in Group E after losing a crucial penultimate game 3-1 to group winners Croatia. Wales were runners-up, only one point ahead. Robert Bozenik and star captain Marek Hamšík were the Slovakians' leading scorers with three goals each.

In the 2018-19 UEFA Nations League Slovakia had finished third in Group B1 behind Ukraine and the Czech Republic. That presented them with a play-off semi-final against the Republic of Ireland. The duel in Bratislava ended goalless after extra time and the Slovakians then converted all their penalties to win the shootout 4-2, sending them on to play Northern Ireland in Belfast.

An early goal from Juraj Kucka meant Slovakia were within two minutes of reaching the finals when an own goal by Milan Škriniar forced them into extra time. They duly regained their composure and command to win 2-1 with a goal after 110 minutes from Michal Ďuriš.

LEFT TO RIGHT: (Back) Milan Škriniar, Denis Vavro, Dávid Hancko, Martin Dúbravka, Juraj Kucka. (Front) Ondrej Duda, Albert Rusnák, Peter Pekarík, Róbert Mak, Marek Hamšík, Stanislav Lobotka.

SLOVAKIA AT THE UEFA EUROPEAN CHAMPIONSHIP

1960	Did not compete
1964	Did not compete
1968	Did not compete
1972	Did not compete
1976	Did not compete
1980	Did not compete
1984	Did not compete
1988	Did not compete
1992	Did not compete
1996	Did not qualify
2000	Did not qualify
2004	Did not qualify
2008	Did not qualify
2012	Did not qualify
2016	Round of 16

COACH

ŠTEFAN TARKOVIČ

Štefan Tarkovič took over as Slovakia coach in between the UEFA EURO 2020 play-off semi-final victory over the Republic of Ireland and ahead of the final against Northern Ireland in Belfast. He succeeded former Czech international Pavel Hapal. However, Tarkovič was no newcomer to the EURO. He was a member of the coaching team under Ján Kozák at the finals in France in 2016. Tarkovič was born on 18 February 1973 in Prešov in the former Czechoslovakia. He played for local club 1.FC Tatran and subsequently coached MŠK Žilina, Tatran and MFK Košice.

STAR PLAYER

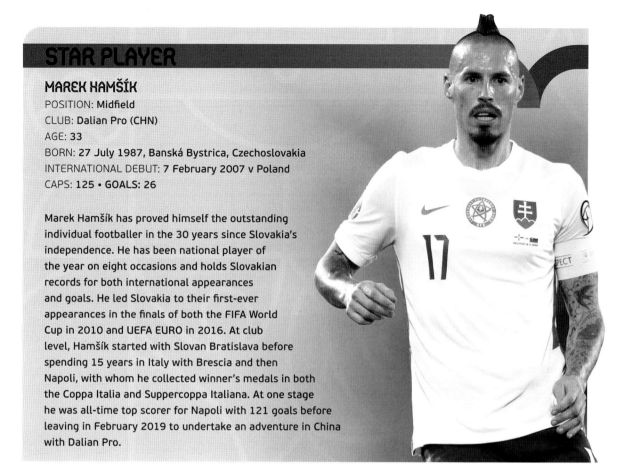

MAREK HAMŠÍK

POSITION: **Midfield**
CLUB: **Dalian Pro (CHN)**
AGE: **33**
BORN: **27 July 1987, Banská Bystrica, Czechoslovakia**
INTERNATIONAL DEBUT: **7 February 2007 v Poland**
CAPS: **125 • GOALS: 26**

Marek Hamšík has proved himself the outstanding individual footballer in the 30 years since Slovakia's independence. He has been national player of the year on eight occasions and holds Slovakian records for both international appearances and goals. He led Slovakia to their first-ever appearances in the finals of both the FIFA World Cup in 2010 and UEFA EURO in 2016. At club level, Hamšík started with Slovan Bratislava before spending 15 years in Italy with Brescia and then Napoli, with whom he collected winner's medals in both the Coppa Italia and Suppercoppa Italiana. At one stage he was all-time top scorer for Napoli with 121 goals before leaving in February 2019 to undertake an adventure in China with Dalian Pro.

Keeping track of a squad scattered around not only Europe but China and the United States has never been a simple task for the Slovakia coaching staff. Even so, Slovakia boast a wealth of international experience with Peter Pekarík, Martin Škrtel and Tomáš Hubočan shoring up the defence, Kucka, Róbert Mak, Ondrej Duda and captain Hamšík in midfield, through to Ďuriš in attack. All had been members of the squad who went to France for the finals five years ago, when they made it out of the group stage.

This generation of Slovakian players will be looking to emulate the proud record of their Czechoslovakian predecessors in the UEFA European Championship. Two third-place finishes, in 1960 and 1980 respectively, and a memorable victory in 1976 set the bar high for future success. The Slovak region specifically played its full part in those Czechoslovakian achievements: no fewer than eight members of the team who won the final of the 1976 UEFA European Championship were Slovak. The Slovan Bratislava club had also earned respect through regular participation in the European club competitions and victory in the now-defunct Cup Winners' Cup in 1969.

Slovakia made their international competitive debut in the qualifiers for EURO '96, but did not appear at a major finals until they reached the FIFA World Cup in South Africa in 2010. Their adventure was brought to a second-round end by a 2-1 defeat against Netherlands.

Six years later, Slovakia returned to the main stage under coach Ján Kozák at UEFA EURO 2016 in France.

A victory over Russia, then a draw with England, secured third place in their group. This meant qualification for the round of 16, where they lost 3-0 to Germany. Now they can draw on that experience to try to reach the knockout stage for a second time in their own right.

DID YOU KNOW?

Slovakia's first international after independence was a 1-0 victory over the United Arab Emirates on 2 February 1994. The goalscorer was Vladimír Weiss, who later became national coach.

2000

MAGIC MOMENTS
Trezeguet the supersub

David Trezeguet capitalised on the golden goal rule to win the ultimate European prize for France. He was the second man to do so in successive finals, after Oliver Bierhoff for Germany against the Czech Republic in 1996. The 2000 finals, in Belgium and the Netherlands, were the first to be co-hosted. Trezeguet opened his account in a group stage defeat by the Netherlands but found himself starting the final against Italy on the substitutes bench. He joined the action in place of Youri Djorkaeff to devastating effect, with only 14 minutes remaining and France losing 1-0. In stoppage time Trezeguet set up an equaliser for Sylvain Wiltord, before bringing the final to a triumphant halt himself from Robert Pirès's assist in extra time.

FINAL
France 2-1 (gg) Italy
Stadion Feijenoord, Rotterdam
2 July 2000

GROUP F

No fewer than three EURO champions provide the drama. Portugal, who kick off against Hungary, are reigning title-holders after their 2016 victory over France, the champions in 1984 and 2000. Germany were crowned a record-equalling three times in 1972, 1980 and 1996.

GROUP F
HUNGARY

Hungary are one of the great historical powers of world football. They reached the last four of the UEFA European Championship in both 1964 and 1972. However, the nation whose old heroes had finished runners-up in the FIFA World Cup in both 1938 and 1954 did not return to the UEFA EURO finals until reaching the round of 16 in France five years ago.

In the 1930s, Hungarians were renowned for their coaching expertise. Hungary's managerial ambassadors took their innovative tactical and technical knowhow all around the world while the likes of Károly Dietz, Gusztáv Sebes, Márton Bukovi, Lajos Baróti, Rudolf Illovszky and György Mezey took the national team to the peaks of the international game.

Most famous of all was the 'Magical Magyars' side under Sebes in the early 1950s. They lost only one

international in five years before falling short at the one match they needed to win most: the 1954 FIFA World Cup final. Stars such as Ferenc Puskás, Sándor Kocsis and József Bozsik still rank among the greatest footballers of all time. In 1953, they became the first non-British Isles side to beat England at home, winning 6-3.

In the 1960s new stars emerged such as Flórián Albert and Ferenc Bene, who led Hungary to the 1962 and 1966 World Cup quarter-finals

COACH

MARCO ROSSI

Marco Rossi, from Druento in north-west Italy, led the Budapest club Honvéd to the Hungarian league title before becoming national manager in June 2018. His playing career as a defender took him from clubs including Italy's Torino, Catanzaro, Brescia and Sampdoria to Mexico's Club América and Germany's Eintracht Frankfurt. Rossi, born on 9 September 1964, returned home to launch his coaching career, then had two spells in Hungary with Honvéd. In between, he spent one season in Slovakia with FC DAC 1904 before returning to succeed Georges Leekens as Hungary coach.

LEFT TO RIGHT: (Back) Ádám Lang, Barnabás Bese, Ádám Szalai, Attila Szalai, Péter Gulácsi, Dominik Szoboszlai. (Front) Willi Orbán, Roland Sallai, Dávid Sigér, Ádám Nagy, Filip Holender.

ÁDÁM SZALAI

POSITION: **Forward**
CLUB: **Mainz (GER)**
AGE: **33**
BORN: **9 December, 1987, Budapest, Hungary**
INTERNATIONAL DEBUT: **11 February 2009 v Israel**
CAPS: **66** • GOALS: **21**

Ádám Szalai has enjoyed a 14-year senior international career in the Hungarian national team even though he has never played his senior club football in his homeland. Szalai, a consistent threat to goal, began with Újpest and Honvéd but moved to Germany at 16 with VfB Stuttgart. His career took him on to Real Madrid before he settled back in German football with Mainz, Schalke, Hoffenheim, Hannover, then Mainz again. He played on more than 20 occasions for Hungary at age-group level before making his senior debut at the age of 21. Szalai scored Hungary's opening goal in the 2-0 defeat of Austria in Bordeaux that kicked off their campaign at the UEFA EURO 2016 finals in France.

and Olympic gold in 1964 and 1968. Later came Tibor Nyilasi, but then the Hungarians slipped into shadows from which they have only recently re-emerged with qualification for UEFA EURO 2016 and 2020.

Hungary managed the latest achievement via the play-offs route. In fact, they could have qualified directly for the finals had they won their last game in the UEFA EURO qualifying competition against Wales in Cardiff. Instead, Balázs Dzsudzsák and his team-mates lost 2-0 and finished fourth in Group E. A lack of attacking firepower had proved costly. Hungary scored only eight times in their eight games with two-goal Willi Orban and Máté Pátkai their joint leading scorers.

Orban, from RB Leipzig, was on target again in Hungary's 3-1 win in Bulgaria in the play-off semi-final. Zsolt Kalmár and Nemanja Nikolić scored the other goals to earn a final

showdown with Iceland back in the new Puskás Arena in Budapest.

An injury-hit team went behind after only 11 minutes, and time was running out when substitute Loïc Négo equalised with two minutes remaining. Dominik Szoboszlai then struck a dramatic winner in the second minute of added time.

Coach Marco Rossi brings to the finals a squad featuring only a handful who undertook the French adventure in 2016. One of them is goalkeeper Péter Gulácsi, who spent five years with Liverpool early in his career without ever appearing in the English Premier League for them. He found regular first-team football after transferring to Salzburg. A further move to RB Leipzig saw him emerge as a key figure in their rise to UEFA Champions League status.

Leipzig club-mate Orban and home-based Gergő Lovrencsics from

Ferencvaros have brought stability to the defence, while midfielder Szoboszlai struck the winning goal in the victory over Iceland after missing the Bulgaria tie.

A central role alongside him in midfield has been taken up by Adam Nagy, another survivor from the 2016 squad. Yet another is Ádám Szalai, who has scored at the rate of a goal every three games since his debut 12 years ago.

DID YOU KNOW?

Hungary played Austria in the first official international match outside the British Isles. The neighbours and old rivals drew 0-0 in Vienna on 12 October 1902.

GROUP F

PORTUGAL

Portugal will be the team to beat at UEFA EURO 2020 as defending champions after their extra-time triumph over France in the Stade de France five years ago. Superstar captain Cristiano Ronaldo and his team-mates then underlined their quality and hunger for more silverware by winning the inaugural UEFA Nations League in front of their own fans last year.

Those successes were long overdue considering the high-profile role Portugal has played in international football. Benfica won the European Champions Clubs' Cup in 1961 and 1962 and provided the backbone of the national team which finished third at the FIFA World Cup in 1966. Their hero was the great Mozambique-born striker Eusébio. He was the tournament's nine-goal leading scorer.

After a 'lost decade' in the 1970s, Portugal revived in the 1980s as Porto won the European Cup and Benfica reached the finals of both that competition and UEFA Cup. A new golden generation won the FIFA World Youth Cups of 1989 and 1991, and star graduate Luís Figo would later be crowned both World and European Player of the Year.

Porto, under José Mourinho, won the UEFA Cup and UEFA Champions

COACH

FERNANDO SANTOS

Fernando Santos, aged 66, is the most successful national team coach in the history of Portuguese football. He guided his side to victory at UEFA EURO 2016 and then in the inaugural UEFA Nations League on home soil last year. Santos never played high-level football, retiring at 21 in 1975 to study electrical engineering. He was lured back by former club Estoril Praia and later coached all the 'big three' of Porto, Sporting CP and Benfica. Santos led Greece to the EURO 2012 quarter-finals before being appointed by Portugal.

LEFT TO RIGHT: (Back) Rúben Neves, Rúben Dias, Gonçalo Paciência, José Fonte, Rui Patrício, Cristiano Ronaldo. (Front) Ricardo Pereira, Bernardo Silva, Mário Rui, Pizzi, Bruno Fernandes.

BERNARDO SILVA

POSITION: **Midfield**
CLUB: **Manchester City (ENG)**
AGE: **26**
BORN: **10 August 1994, Lisbon, Portugal**
INTERNATIONAL DEBUT: **31 March 2015 v Cape Verde**
CAPS: **51 • GOALS: 7**

Bernardo Mota Veiga de Carvalho e Silva was marked out for high-profile success ever since his teenage days in the Benfica youth academy. He was promoted to the first team in 2014 and starred as playmaker of the Portuguese team who were runners-up at the European Under-21s a year later. By then Silva had moved to French football with Monaco and led them to victory in the French league in 2017. Manchester City bought him for €50m and he won the Premier League and Football League Cup in the next two seasons, as well as the FA Cup to complete a unique treble in 2019. Silva missed UEFA EURO 2016 through injury, but was voted best player in Portugal's UEFA Nations League success in 2019.

League in 2003 and 2004 to spark a renewal of confidence in the national team. They finished runners-up as hosts at UEFA EURO 2004 and then took fourth place at the 2006 FIFA World Cup. A new young inspiration in Cristiano Ronaldo would develop into one of the greatest footballers and goalscorers of all time.

In France, at UEFA EURO 2016, Ronaldo urged his team-mates on to victory from the technical area after being substituted because of injury early in the final.

Ronaldo was on target with 11 goals in the preliminary competition for UEFA EURO 2020 in which Portugal had been drawn against Lithuania, Luxembourg and Ukraine. They won five of their eight games to qualify as runners-up behind Ukraine. Ronaldo scored the ninth hat-trick

of his national team career in a 6-0 defeat of Lithuania. This victory sealed Portugal's place in the finals with one group match to spare. That last tie was a 2-0 win in Luxembourg, in which Ronaldo scored his 99th international goal.

In the middle of the qualifying campaign Portugal became the first winners of the UEFA Nations League. They had topped a group featuring Italy and Poland, then capitalised on home advantage in Porto in the finals. Portugal beat Switzerland 3-1 in the semi-finals with a Ronaldo hat-trick and followed up by defeating Netherlands 1-0 in the final.

Opponents at UEFA EURO 2020 would be mistaken to consider Portugal as a one-man team. Goalkeeper Rui Patrício has played around 90 times for his country

since his debut ten years ago, while defenders José Fonte and Raphaël Guerreiro are other veterans of the triumphant 2016 campaign. In midfield the experience of João Moutinho is complemented by the energy of Bernardo Silva. Then, in attack, of course, there is always Ronaldo.

DID YOU KNOW?

The 2-1 loss to Ukraine in October 2019 was the first Portugal have suffered under Fernando Santos in a EURO or Nations League game – qualifier or final tournament – since he took charge.

GROUP F
FRANCE

France have a proud history on and off the pitch. Frenchmen such as Robert Guérin, Jules Rimet, Henri Delaunay and Gabriel Hanot played crucial roles, respectively, in the creation of world federation FIFA, the World Cup, European federation UEFA and its European Championship, as well as what is now the UEFA Champions League.

Out on the pitch it was a Frenchman, Lucien Laurent, who scored the very first goal in the inaugural FIFA World Cup, and France who hosted the first European Championship, then known as the Nations' Cup, in 1960. Les Bleus finished fourth that time but more than made amends the next time they played host, in 1984.

France defeated Spain 2-0 in the final in the Parc des Princes in Paris. Victory for the first time was achieved thanks in particular to the top-scoring nine-goal inspiration of captain Michel Platini. He was national coach when France appeared at the 1992 finals and then FIFA World Cup organising president in 1998. France won then, as hosts, and followed up with a second EURO triumph in neighbouring Belgium and Holland two years later amid intense drama. In the semi-final they defeated Portugal thanks to a late, extra-time penalty from Zinedine Zidane, then followed up in the final

COACH

DIDIER DESCHAMPS

Didier Deschamps knows all about the pressures of national team competition as both player and coach. The former Marseille, Juventus and Chelsea midfielder led France to FIFA World Cup victory as captain in 1998 and then as coach in 2018. He also captained Les Bleus to EURO success in 2000. Deschamps coached Monaco, Juventus and Marseille before he took over France in 2012. His one major setback was seeing his team finish runners-up to Portugal in front of their own supporters at the Stade de France five years ago.

LEFT TO RIGHT: (Back) Clément Lenglet, Benjamin Pavard, Lucas Hernandez, Raphaël Varane, Olivier Giroud, Hugo Lloris. (Front) Antoine Griezmann, Corentin Tolisso, Blaise Matuidi, Thomas Lemar, Kingsley Coman.

STAR PLAYER

ANTOINE GRIEZMANN

POSITION: **Striker**
CLUB: **Barcelona (ESP)**
AGE: **30**
BORN: **21 March 1991, Mâcon, France**
INTERNATIONAL DEBUT: **11 August 2014 v Netherlands**
CAPS: **86** • GOALS: **33**

Antoine Griezmann, one of European football's most lethal strikers, has played all his club football in Spain, with Real Sociedad, Atlético Madrid and now Barcelona. He made his senior France debut in spring 2014 and became six-goal leading scorer and player of the tournament when the hosts finished runners-up at UEFA EURO 2016. The most outstanding year of his career was 2018. First Griezmann helped Atlético win the UEFA Europa League, scoring twice in their victory over Marseille in the final. Weeks later he scored four goals in Russia when France won the FIFA World Cup. One year on, Griezmann became the fourth most expensive player of all time in leaving Atlético for Barcelona for €120m.

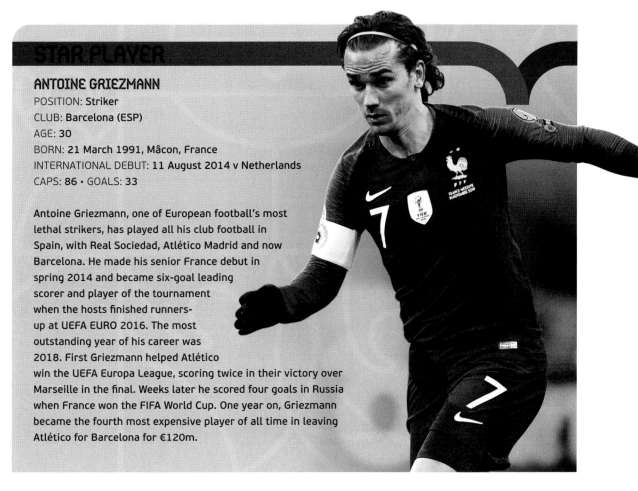

by beating Italy with an extra-time golden goal from David Trezeguet.

Didier Deschamps, now the national coach, was captain of the team which won both the World Cup and then the European title.

Six years later, in 2006, France finished runners-up on penalties to Italy at the 2006 FIFA World Cup. They were runners-up again, as hosts, at UEFA EURO 2016, but made amends two years later in defeating Croatia 4-2 to win the final of the FIFA World Cup in Russia. The tournament saw the explosive emergence of a new young superstar in Kylian Mbappé.

Deschamps has been able to rely on a solid backbone to his team, starting with goalkeeper Hugo Lloris. He first made his name in helping France win the European Under-19 title in 2005. Three times he was voted goalkeeper of the year while progressing with Nice and Lyon, before moving to the English Premier League with Tottenham Hotspur in 2012.

In front of him, Real Madrid's Raphael Varane is one of the classiest central defenders in the European game. Varane is not only a world champion, but a four-time winner of the UEFA Champions League. Ahead of them is a solid midfield commanded by N'Golo Kanté and Paul Pogba, then an attack that features Mbappé, Antoine Griezmann and Olivier Giroud.

France qualified by finishing top of Group H, two points ahead of Turkey, who pursued them right through to the last matchday. Their one defeat was suffered against the Turkish, 2-0 in Konya in June last year. The return ended in a 1-1 draw in the Stade de France, which left Deschamps' men needing to win their last game to finish first and join the top seeds. France duly won 2-0 in Albania and Giroud ended as the group's six-goal leading marksman.

DID YOU KNOW?

If France are victorious at EURO 2020, they will become only the fourth team to hold both the FIFA World Cup and European Championship titles simultaneously.

GROUP F

GERMANY

Germany demonstrated in qualifying that they are back on track after a time of transition. The loss of their FIFA World Cup crown in Russia in 2018 had been followed by a disappointing campaign in the UEFA Nations League. But a rebuilt team found form and finesse in launching their pursuit of a first EURO success since 1996.

Coach Joachim Löw has continued to benefit from the defensive experience of senior players such as goalkeeper and captain Manuel Neuer, plus Antonio Rüdiger and Matthias Ginter. Further forward, Joshua Kimmich and Toni Kroos are among the world game's most admired midfielders, aided and abetted by İlkay Gündoğan and Leon Goretzka.

In attack, the challenge for Löw had been to find effective successors to old favourites such as Miroslav Klose and Thomas Müller. The evidence of the qualifiers and subsequent UEFA Nations League is that he has achieved that with the emergence of the explosive Serge Gnabry and Timo Werner, with dangerous support from Julian Draxler, Leroy Sané and Kai Havertz.

The challenge for Germany in Group C was presented by Belarus, Estonia, Netherlands and Northern

COACH

JOACHIM LÖW

Joachim 'Jogi' Löw was Jürgen Klinsmann's assistant when Germany finished third at the 2006 FIFA World Cup finals and succeeded him as coach afterwards. Löw, born on 3 February 3 1960, had previously bossed VfB Stuttgart and Karlsruhe, Turkey's Fenerbahçe and Adanaspor, plus Austria's Tirol Innsbruck and Austria Wien. He immediately led Germany to the UEFA EURO 2008 final, then rebuilt a team that won the FIFA World Cup in 2014 either side of reaching two EURO semi-finals in Ukraine/Poland and then France.

LEFT TO RIGHT: (Back) Manuel Neuer, Toni Kroos, Leon Goretzka, Robin Koch, Matthias Ginter, Lukas Klostermann. (Front) Nico Schulz, İlkay Gündoğan, Serge Gnabry, Joshua Kimmich, Timo Werner.

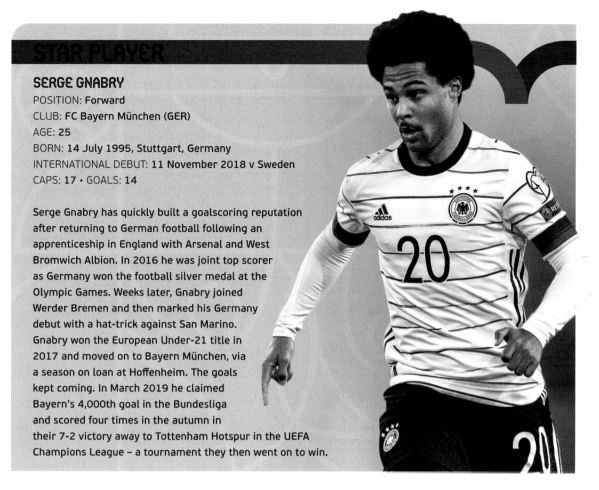

STAR PLAYER

SERGE GNABRY

POSITION: **Forward**
CLUB: **FC Bayern München (GER)**
AGE: **25**
BORN: **14 July 1995, Stuttgart, Germany**
INTERNATIONAL DEBUT: **11 November 2018 v Sweden**
CAPS: **17** • GOALS: **14**

Serge Gnabry has quickly built a goalscoring reputation after returning to German football following an apprenticeship in England with Arsenal and West Bromwich Albion. In 2016 he was joint top scorer as Germany won the football silver medal at the Olympic Games. Weeks later, Gnabry joined Werder Bremen and then marked his Germany debut with a hat-trick against San Marino. Gnabry won the European Under-21 title in 2017 and moved on to Bayern München, via a season on loan at Hoffenheim. The goals kept coming. In March 2019 he claimed Bayern's 4,000th goal in the Bundesliga and scored four times in the autumn in their 7-2 victory away to Tottenham Hotspur in the UEFA Champions League – a tournament they then went on to win.

Ireland. This meant an immediate opening rematch with the Dutch side to whom the Germans had lost 3-0 in the UEFA Nations League. This time Germany came out on top, winning 3-2 in Amsterdam via goals from Leroy Sané, Gnabry and Nico Schulz in the last minute.

A subsequent 4-2 defeat by Netherlands in Hamburg proved the only match in which Germany dropped points. They won all their other seven games and wrapped up their campaign with a 6-1 defeat of Northern Ireland in Frankfurt. The goal-hungry Gnabry scored a hat-trick. He ended as the group's eight-goal joint top scorer with Dutchman Georginio Wijnaldum.

Germany will be among the favourites in the finals on the basis of not only their qualifying form, but their proven status as winners of the FIFA World Cup four times and of the UEFA European Championship on three occasions. Yet they made a slow start in pursuit of the Henri Delaunay trophy. They did not enter the 1960 and 1964 championships and were eliminated in the first round in the 1968 qualifying competition.

Everything changed in the 1970s. Bayern München won a hat-trick of European Cups in 1974, 1975 and 1976, and provided the nucleus of the national side who won the EURO in 1972, the FIFA World Cup in 1974, and after finishing second in 1976, the European title again in 1980.

Franz Beckenbauer revolutionised the sweeper's role into one of attack as well as defence, while Gerd Müller was a scoring machine with 68 goals in 62 internationals. Later heroes included Karl-Heinz Rummenigge,

Lothar Matthäus and Rudi Völler. Jürgen Klinsmann was one of the stars of the team who won the FIFA World Cup in 1990 and EURO '96 after German reunification.

That was their last senior title until the dramatic FIFA World Cup victory over Argentina in 2014, which featured a last-minute strike from Mario Götze.

DID YOU KNOW?

EURO 2020 will be Germany's 26th successive major tournament, namely the FIFA World Cup or European Championship.

MAGIC MOMENTS
Greece surprise winners

Greece sprang the greatest surprise since Denmark in 1992 by winning the European crown in Portugal. Even more remarkable, they did so by defeating the hosts in front of their own fans in Lisbon in the final. Veteran German coach Otto Rehhagel brought organisation and discipline to a Greek national team which had never previously won even one match at a major finals. They sounded a warning by defeating Portugal 2-1 in the group stage on their way to the knockout rounds. Here they overcame holders France, then defeated the Czech Republic on the experimental silver goal system in the semi-finals. A third successive single-goal victory spelled triumph in the final, courtesy of a second-half header from centre-forward Angelos Charisteas.

FINAL
Portugal 0-**1 Greece**
Estádio da Luz, Lisbon
4 July 2004

EURO 2020 SUPERSTARS

The finals of the UEFA European Championship are a perfect platform for the established stars of the international game to burnish their reputations, and for a new generation to make their names. The line-up of superstars heading for the finals features a wide range of talents from all over the pitch, from commanding defenders to creative midfielders and lethal forwards.

GARETH BALE

Gareth Bale is the most decorated footballer in the Welsh game. Wales' captain was one of their outstanding players in the run to the semi-finals of UEFA EURO 2016 in France. He has also won 13 world and European club prizes with Spanish giants Real Madrid before returning to Tottenham Hotspur. Bale was the FIFA Club World Cup's top scorer in both 2014 and 2018.

BORN: 16 July 1989
POSITION: Forward
CLUBS: Southampton (ENG), Tottenham Hotspur (ENG), Real Madrid (ESP), Tottenham (ENG)
CAPS (GOALS): 87 (33)

Bale, born in Cardiff, made his name as a teenager with Southampton, but as a left-back rather than as a forward. It was only after transferring to Tottenham in 2007 that he was transformed under the managership of Harry Redknapp into a wide-ranging goalscoring winger. Bale first lit up the UEFA Champions League with a hat-trick against Internazionale in a group stage tie in 2010.

Three years later he was voted player of the year in the English game by both his fellow players and by the media. That summer of 2013 saw Bale transferred to Real Madrid for a then-world record €100m. The pinnacle of his club career was a match-winning two-goal performance as a substitute in Madrid's UEFA Champions League victory over Liverpool in 2018.

Bale became Wales' youngest-ever senior international in May 2006. In 2018 he scored a hat-trick against China to overtake 28-goal Ian Rush as his country's all-time leading marksman. He was their seven-goal top scorer in their EURO 2016 qualifying campaign and scored a further three in the finals.

RIGHT: Already a hero to Welsh fans, Gareth Bale will aim to emulate his nation's improbable success at EURO 2016.

LEONARDO BONUCCI

Leonardo Bonucci has been a defensive pillar in the Italian national team and Serie A for more than a decade. He began with hometown Viterbese, spent various seasons out on loan and then established himself at Bari in 2009/10. His fine form prompted a move to Juventus, with whom he has won eight league titles, interrupted by one season with Milan. At Juve, Bonucci's partnership with Andrea Barzagli and Giorgio Chiellini earned the trio the nickname of 'BBC'.

BORN: 1 May 1987
POSITION: Central defender
CLUBS: Internazionale (ITA),
Genoa (ITA), Bari (ITA),
Juventus (ITA), Milan (ITA),
Juventus (ITA)
CAPS (GOALS): 99 (7)

Bonucci is both solid and quick on the ground and commanding in the air. Those qualities have served Italy well over the decade since his debut against Cameroon in a friendly in 2010. Subsequently Bonucci starred at the 2010 and 2014 FIFA World Cups as well as the 2012 and 2016 UEFA European Championship finals. With Italy he was a EURO runner-up in Poland and Ukraine eight years ago. The Azzurri lost to holders Spain in the final.

Individual honours include the Serie A Footballer of the Year award in 2016 as well as selection for the UEFA Europa League squad of the season in 2014 and 2018. He also featured in the UEFA Fans' Team of the Year in 2016.

Last November Bonucci made his 95th national team appearance against Armenia to overtake old Internazionale hero Giacinto Facchetti and become the ninth most-capped Italian player of all time. Manchester City manager Pep Guardiola has described Bonucci as one of his "most favourite-ever players."

RIGHT: Leonardo Bonucci will attempt to translate his domestic dominance into an international winner's medal at EURO 2020.

DAVID DE GEA

David de Gea knows all about being a European champion. He was captain of the Spanish team which won the UEFA European Under-21 Championship in 2011 and 2013. After that double success he stepped up to the senior team as reserve, and then successor, to the iconic Iker Casillas.

BORN: 7 November 1990
POSITION: Goalkeeper
CLUBS: Atlético Madrid (ESP),
Manchester United (ENG)
CAPS: 45

De Gea was born in Madrid, where he was discovered by Atlético at age 13. Five years later he made his breakthrough in La Liga and became a key figure in the team that won both the UEFA Europa League and the UEFA Super Cup in 2010. A year later, Manchester United took him to the English Premier League for £19m, then a British record for a goalkeeper.

National coach Vicente del Bosque handed De Gea his Spain debut as a substitute in a friendly against El Salvador shortly before the FIFA World Cup in 2014. De Gea was selected as back-up to Casillas and Pepe Reina – he was the only member of the squad not to play a minute in Brazil. Three months later he made his first start in a 1-0 defeat by France in Paris. Subsequently, De Gea became Spain's No1 goalkeeper at the finals of UEFA EURO 2016 and the FIFA World Cup in Russia two years later.

Simultaneously, he had also established himself as a favourite with Manchester United fans. They voted him their player of the season on four occasions as he anchored successes in UEFA Europa League, Premier League, FA Cup and League Cup.

RIGHT: David de Gea will look to replicate his success in the Under-21s at EURO 2020.

CHRISTIAN ERIKSEN

Christian Eriksen was the youngest player on view, aged 18, at the FIFA World Cup in 2010 in South Africa and has fulfilled all his early teenage promise. One year later his creative talents and eye for a goal from midfield saw him become a Dutch champion with Ajax. He collected the first of his five Danish Footballer of the Year awards, was voted Eredevisie Talent of the Year and was nominated for the Under-21 finals Team of the Tournament.

BORN: 14 February 1992
POSITION: Midfielder
CLUBS: Ajax (NED),
Tottenham Hotspur (ENG),
Internazionale (ITA)
CAPS (GOALS): 103 (36)

Eriksen had begun in the academy of his hometown club Middelfart where his father, Thomas, was one of the coaches. He moved on up with Odense Boldklub before joining Ajax in the Netherlands in 2008. Two more years and he was making his debut for the Ajax senior team. Four Eredivisie titles followed in the next five years.

Simultaneously, Eriksen progressed up through the Danish national youth teams before making his senior debut against Austria in March 2010. At little more than 18 he was the youngest debutant since Michael Laudrup. Eriksen went on to the World Cup, where he played in two games, only for Denmark to fall in the group stage.

Eriksen had been scouted by many of Europe's leading clubs ever since his youth days and one of them, Tottenham, bought him for £11m in 2013. He won the club's player of the year prize in 2014 and 2017 and was a key member of the team that reached the UEFA Champions League final in 2019, before moving to Italy with Internazionale in 2020.

Eriksen can not only make goals but also score them. He struck 11 times in Denmark's qualifying campaign for the 2018 FIFA World Cup, and five times on their road to the UEFA EURO 2020 finals.

RIGHT: Christian Eriksen is Denmark's talisman, and boasts an impressive scoring record for his country.

EDEN HAZARD

Eden Hazard is one of the most electric forwards in world football. His explosive acceleration and close control has thrilled crowds in France, England, Spain and his native Belgium.

BORN: 7 January 1991
POSITION: Forward
CLUBS: Lille (FRA),
Chelsea (ENG),
Real Madrid (ESP)
CAPS (GOALS): 106 (32)

Yet Hazard never played professional football in the homeland whose national team he captains. Instead, the son of parents who were both footballers began his senior career across the north-western border in France with Lille. He made his league debut at 16 and was twice voted Young Player of the Year before leading Lille to double success in the French league and cup in 2011.

One year later Hazard was transferred to London club Chelsea. In an outstanding seven-year spell he helped inspire trophy-winning success in the UEFA Europa League, Premier League, FA Cup and League Cup. On an individual level he was hailed in 2015 as player of the year by both journalists and his fellow players.

Hazard was still only 17 when he followed up Belgian youth international appearances by making his debut for the senior team against Luxembourg in November 2008. He had to wait three years for his first international goal, against Kazakhstan, but has followed up with many more since.

Belgium, with Hazard an established starter, reached the quarter-finals of the FIFA World Cup in 2014, UEFA EURO 2016 and then finished third at the 2018 FIFA World Cup. By now Hazard's inspirational qualities had seen him appointed captain of his country, and they soon prompted Real Madrid to agree a reported €100m deal to buy him from Chelsea.

RIGHT: As captain of Belgium's 'Golden Generation', Eden Hazard has a chance to lead the Red Devils to their first major honour.

HARRY KANE

Harry Kane is the latest in a long line of fine England marksmen, from Dixie Dean to Tommy Lawton, Geoff Hurst and Alan Shearer. Kane scored in each of England's eight qualifying matches en route to UEFA EURO 2020. He claimed his third hat-trick in the 7-0 victory over Montenegro, which secured England's place in the finals in their 1,000th international.

BORN: 28 July 1993
POSITION: Centre-forward
CLUBS: Tottenham Hotspur (ENG)
CAPS (GOALS): 51 (32)

A further goal in England's concluding 4-0 win over Kosovo established him as the 12-goal overall top scorer in the qualifiers. The goal was also his 32nd for his country, lifting him to sixth in England's all-time list. He thus overtook old heroes Tom Finney, Nat Lofthouse and Shearer, all on 30.

Kane's achievements maintained a remarkable goal-scoring pattern. He scored at every international youth level and then on his senior debut in March 2015 against Lithuania. Kane did not find the net at EURO 2016 but made amends at the FIFA World Cup in 2018. England finished fourth and their newly-appointed captain finished as the tournament's six-goal leading marksman.

As a boy, Kane joined Tottenham after being released by Arsenal. He turned professional in 2010 and had loan spells with four other clubs before returning to make his Spurs Premier League debut in April 2014. Since then he has scored more than 180 goals in all competitions and twice been the league's top scorer. Kane scored four goals in leading Tottenham to the UEFA Champions League final in 2019.

RIGHT: Harry Kane has both the Golden Boot and EURO 2020 glory in sight.

MAGIC MOMENTS
Spain's treble triumph

Spain, with their mesmerising tiki-taka possession football, commanded the world and European game between 2008 and 2012. La Roja won EURO titles in 2008 and 2012, as well as the FIFA World Cup in between in 2010. Veteran coach Luis Aragonés plotted the victorious 2008 campaign in Austria and Switzerland, which climaxed in a 1-0 victory over Germany in Vienna. Fernando Torres was the match-winner. Aragonés then retired, so Vicente del Bosque guided Spain to success at the FIFA World Cup in South Africa and then to a European repeat in Ukraine and Poland in 2012. Torres was again on the scoresheet, but this time the margin of victory was more decisive. He added to early strikes from David Silva and Jordi Alba, before Juan Mata capped off a 4-0 victory over Italy.

FINAL
Spain 4-0 Italy
NSK Olimpiyskyi, Kyiv
1 July 2012

TONI KROOS

Toni Kroos is one of the most dominant and admired playmakers in the modern game after his successes at the highest levels with the German national team, and with Bayern Munich and Real Madrid in club football.

BORN: 4 January 1990
POSITION: Midfield
CLUBS: Bayern Munich (GER),
Bayer Leverkusen (GER),
Real Madrid (ESP)
CAPS (GOALS): 101 (17)

Kroos was born and brought up in Greifswald in the north-east of what was still then the German Democratic Republic. He started with the local club then entered the youth section of Hansa Rostock. In 2006 Kroos, still only 16, moved west to join the Bayern Munich academy. A year later his evident talent earned him a Bundesliga debut as a substitute in a 5-0 win over Energie Cottbus.

An 18-month loan to Bayer Leverkusen followed, after which Kroos returned in 2010 to Bayern and became an established first-team starter before transferring to Real Madrid in 2014. Kroos won nine national and international trophies with Bayern and has added a further 11 since moving to Spain. He is a four-times winner of the UEFA Champions League, once with Bayern and three times with Real Madrid.

Kroos carried his club form into the national team. He won the golden ball as best player at the 2007 FIFA U-17 World Cup and made his debut for the senior team in a friendly against Argentina in March 2010. He made three appearances in the FIFA World Cup in South Africa, where Germany finished third, and was one of the stars of the tournament when Germany won the 2014 finals in Brazil. He was also a member of the team which reached the EURO semi-finals in both 2012 and 2016.

RIGHT: Now a veteran performer for club and country, Toni Kroos remains at the top of his game.

SEBASTIAN LARSSON

Sebastian Larsson is a set-piece specialist and forceful midfielder who has been an established member of the Swedish national team ever since making his debut in 2008. Yet he did not play senior football in his home country until he joined AIK in 2018. Up until then Larsson had played all his professional club football in England.

BORN: 6 June 1985
POSITION: Midfielder
CLUBS: Arsenal (ENG),
Birmingham City (ENG),
Sunderland (ENG),
Hull City (ENG), AIK (SWE)
CAPS (GOALS): 125 (8)

Larsson, born in Eskilstuna, was scouted as a teenager by Arsenal and was sent, on loan initially, to Birmingham City where he stayed for five years before moving on to the north-east of England with Sunderland and then Hull City. He was a League Cup winner with Birmingham in 2011 and runner-up with Sunderland in 2014.

All the while, Larsson was building a reputation in international football with Sweden. He played more than 40 times with the under-17s, under-19s and under-21s before making his debut in a draw against Turkey in a friendly international in February 2008. Larsson's energy and pace earned him selection months later for the EURO finals in Austria and Switzerland.

Sweden – and Larsson – were eliminated in the group phase both then and again, four years later, at the finals in Poland and Ukraine. Sweden were absent from the finals in France in 2016 but qualified for the 2018 FIFA World Cup in Russia. Larsson won his 100th cap for his country in their last warm-up game, a draw with Peru. He then made four appearances at the finals, in which Sweden reached the quarter-finals before losing to England.

RIGHT: Sebastian Larsson's experience will be key if Sweden are to progress at EURO 2020.

ROBERT LEWANDOWSKI

Robert Lewandowski's insatiable hunger for goals has been evident ever since his very first appearance for Poland, when he marked his debut against San Marino with the first of more than 60 goals over the years.

BORN: 21 August 1988
POSITION: Forward
CLUBS: Znicz Pruszków (POL),
Lech Poznań (POL),
Borussia Dortmund (GER),
Bayern Munich (GER)
CAPS (GOALS): 116 (63)

That tally represents a record for his nation, far outstripping past heroes such as 1970s stars Wlodzimierz Lubanski (48 goals), Grzegorz Lato (45) and Kazimierz Deyna (41). Along the way he struck the first goal at UEFA EURO 2012, which Poland co-hosted with Ukraine. He then equalled the EURO qualifying goals record with 13 in the run-up to the 2016 finals. He followed up with a remarkable 16 in qualifying for the 2018 FIFA World Cup in Russia.

Lewandowski, exceptionally quick for a man of his height, first made the Polish game take notice when, as a teenager, he was leading marksman in both third and second divisions with Znicz Pruszków. A 2008 transfer to Lech Poznań saw him win the league, cup, super cup and another top-scorer prize, which secured a move to Germany with Borussia Dortmund in 2010.

Goals and glory followed to the tune of two Bundesliga titles, one German Cup and a runners-up medal in the UEFA Champions League, before a further move to Bayern Munich resulted in 2020 Champions League success and six more league titles. He was 15-goal top scorer in the 2019-20 Champions League and has finished as the leading Bundesliga marksman five times in seven seasons between 2014 and 2020.

RIGHT: Can Robert Lewandowski continue his record-breaking form for Poland?

KYLIAN MBAPPÉ

Kylian Mbappé is one of the most exciting young players to have exploded on the European game for many years. His pace and power in attack have provided an added dimension to both the French national team and to his current club, champions Paris Saint-Germain. He was acclaimed as best young player after France's victory at the 2018 FIFA World Cup.

BORN: 20 December 1998
POSITION: Forward
CLUBS: Monaco (FRA),
Paris Saint-Germain (FRA)
CAPS (GOALS): 39 (16)

Mbappé was born in Paris and took his first steps in football in the suburban Paris club Bondy where his father, Wilfried, was a coach. His talent brought a move to the Clairefontaine national academy and attracted scouts and offers from leading clubs in England, Germany and Spain. Eventually he accepted at offer from Monaco, where he became their youngest debutant at 16 years 347 days.

Goals and even hat-tricks followed as Mbappé's star shone ever more brightly in French domestic competitions as well as in the UEFA Champions League. Mbappé's goals led Monaco to the semi-finals in 2017, after which he joined PSG, initially on loan, and subsequently for €150m. Thus he became the second-most expensive player of all time.

Mbappé lived up to the status by helping PSG win the league, league cup and national cup while simultaneously starring on his FIFA World Cup debut. In Russia, Mbappé became the youngest French player to score at a World Cup and the second teenager, after Brazil's Pelé 60 years earlier, to score in a World Cup final. His four goals saw him end as the tournament's joint second-top marksman.

RIGHT: Kylian Mbappé is ready to ignite on the international stage once again at EURO 2020.

LUKA MODRIĆ

Luka Modrić, Croatia's captain and playmaker, knows all about success at international level after winning the UEFA Champions League on four occasions and 12 other national and international trophies with Real Madrid. Previously Modrić had been three times a league champion and twice a national cup winner in Croatia with Dinamo Zagreb.

BORN: 9 September 1985
POSITION: Midfielder
CLUBS: Dinamo Zagreb (CRO),
  Zrinjski Mostar (CRO),
  Inter Zapresic (CRO),
  Tottenham Hotspur (ENG),
  Real Madrid (ESP)
CAPS (GOALS): 133 (16)

The pinnacle of Modrić's 15-year national team career was leading Croatia to the final of the 2018 FIFA World Cup in Russia, where they finished runners-up to France. It was the closest Croatia had come to seizing one of the major national team prizes. But, with Modrić commanding their midfield, they have always been among the most threatening challengers.

Modrić was playing for Dinamo Zagreb when he was called up first for the national team against Argentina in March 2006. Three months later he made two appearances as a substitute at the FIFA World Cup in Germany where Croatia tumbled out at the group stage. Modrić was then at the heart of the action when the Croatians reached the quarter-finals at UEFA EURO 2008.

Croatia failed to progress beyond the group stage in 2012 and also at the FIFA World Cup in 2014. They then reached the round of 16 at UEFA EURO 2016 in France, where Modrić became the first Croatian to score a goal in two European finals tournaments. He took over as captain for the 2018 World Cup campaign, when he was acclaimed as the best player at the tournament.

RIGHT: Luka Modrić has consistently dazzled for Croatia, and will look to do so once again.

CRISTIANO RONALDO

Cristiano Ronaldo dos Santos Aveiro ranks as one of the greatest players in football history through his stand-alone achievements at national team, club and individual levels. Portugal's captain has claimed a host of world player awards among a plethora of prizes which have seen him win the FIFA Club World Cup four times, the UEFA Champions League five times – both with Manchester United and Real Madrid – the UEFA European Championship in 2016 and the inaugural UEFA Nations League in 2019.

BORN: 5 February 1985
POSITION: Forward
CLUBS: Sporting Club (POR),
Manchester United (ENG),
Real Madrid (ESP),
Juventus (ITA)
CAPS (GOALS): 170 (102)

The Madeira-born forward now claims more than 600 goals in a lethal 19-year career bringing him from Sporting Club of Lisbon to pinnacles of the club game in England, Spain and Italy. He has set marksmanship records, including a stream of hat-tricks, in the Champions League and the Spanish league.

On the way he has outstripped the goalscoring achievements of Portugal's 1960s legend Eusébio. His status was officially recognised in 2015 when he was named as the best Portuguese player of all time by his football association.

Ronaldo was 18 in August 2003 when he made his international debut against Kazakhstan. He now ranks as record-holder in terms of both international appearances and goals. Ronaldo has also led Portugal into the finals of nine major tournaments, starting with EURO 2004 when they finished runners-up as hosts. In France, 12 years later, Ronaldo scored three goals and was an inspiration from the touchline after being injured early in Portugal's final victory over the hosts.

RIGHT: EURO 2020 could see Cristiano Ronaldo become the all-time top scorer at the UEFA European Championship.

XHERDAN SHAQIRI

Xherdan Shaqiri's skill, pace and eye for goal have earned him a string of trophies in Switzerland, Germany and England. He was also a UEFA European Under-21 Championship runner-up in 2011 with Switzerland, which had been his home since his family left eastern Kosovo when he was a year old.

BORN: 10 October 1991
POSITION: Winger
CLUBS: Basel (SUI),
Bayern Munich (GER),
Internazionale (ITA),
Stoke City (ENG),
Liverpool (ENG)
CAPS (GOALS): 84 (22)

Shaqiri was first noted at only eight by Basel, with whom he turned professional in 2009. A year later he made his debut for Switzerland against Uruguay in March 2010. Coach Ottmar Hitzfeld included him in the squad at the FIFA World Cup and, four years later, he scored a hat-trick against Honduras as the 'Nati' reached the round of 16 in Brazil.

The last 16 was also the end of the road for Shaqiri and Switzerland on his first appearance at the EURO finals in 2016 in France. He remained a key member of the team that reached the finals of the FIFA World Cup in 2018 and the UEFA Nations League in 2019. Shaqiri was named in the Team of the Tournament in Portugal.

At club level, Shaqiri's skill and goals brought him three Swiss league titles and two national cups with Basel before he moved to Bayern Munich. Further success followed in the UEFA Champions League in 2013 and in the Bundesliga and German cup before Shaqiri moved to the English Premier League with Stoke City. He joined Liverpool in 2018 and shared in their subsequent UEFA Champions League and Premier League successes.

RIGHT: Xherdan Shaqiri provided some truly spectacular moments at UEFA EURO 2016.

VIRGIL VAN DIJK

Virgil van Dijk is a goalscoring inspiration from central defence with both the Netherlands and Liverpool. The past three years of Van Dijk's career have seen him secure an international reputation and add further lustre to an impressive career curriculum vitae.

BORN: 8 July, 1991
POSITION: Central defender
CLUBS: Groningen (NED),
Celtic (SCO),
Southampton (ENG),
Liverpool (ENG)
CAPS (GOALS): 38 (4)

In 2019 Van Dijk helped Liverpool win their first UEFA Champions League crown in 15 years against Tottenham Hotspur in Madrid. Just over a week later he led the Netherlands to the final of the inaugural UEFA Nations League, where they finished runners-up to hosts Portugal.

Jürgen Klopp, Van Dijk's club manager, said he could not remember any defender having a more impressive season than the Dutchman in 2018/19. He then went on to inspire them to a first English league title in 30 years in 2020.

Van Dijk, born in Breda, played at youth level with Willem II and then Groningen. His early career was interrupted by serious illness but he recovered to fulfil his early promise and was sold in 2013 to Scottish champions Celtic. Two years later, Van Dijk flew south to the English Premier League to join Southampton. A transfer to Liverpool in January 2018 for £75m was then a world record for a defender.

After rising through the under-19s and under-21s, Van Dijk made his senior Netherlands debut against Kazakhstan in October 2015 in the EURO qualifying competition. The Dutch did not qualify for the finals or for the FIFA World Cup in 2018. Van Dijk, now captain, will thus be leading them into their first EURO finals since the group stage finish in 2012.

RIGHT: The brilliant Virgil van Dijk has been one of the catalysts behind the Netherlands' return to the EURO.

2016

MAGIC MOMENTS
Ronaldo leads from the front

Cristiano Ronaldo added the EURO crown to his record-breaking string of honours, as Portugal defeated hosts France after extra time in Saint-Denis. But Ronaldo's role in the final was restricted mostly to one of exhortation from the bench and technical advice, after early injury forced him off the pitch. In his absence it was substitute Éder who scored the lone winning goal in the second half of extra time. But Ronaldo had made his presence felt earlier in the finals. He scored twice in a group stage draw with Hungary which edged Portugal into the knockout stage, converted his penalty in a shootout victory over Poland in the quarter-finals, and struck the first goal in a 2-0 semi-final defeat of Wales.

FINAL
Portugal 1-0 (aet) France
Stade de France, Saint-Denis
10 July 2016

UEFA EURO 2020 Match Schedule

Fill in the results as the tournament unfolds and find out if your fancied teams for the finals live up to your expectations.

GROUP A

11 June, 21:00	Turkey	☐☐	Italy	Rome
12 June, 15:00	Wales	☐☐	Switzerland	Baku
16 June, 18:00	Turkey	☐☐	Wales	Baku
16 June, 21:00	Italy	☐☐	Switzerland	Rome
20 June, 18:00	Italy	☐☐	Wales	Rome
20 June, 18:00	Switzerland	☐☐	Turkey	Baku

Team	P	W	D	L	GD	Pts
1						
2						
3						
4						

GROUP B

12 June, 18:00	Denmark	☐☐	Finland	Copenhagen
12 June, 21:00	Belgium	☐☐	Russia	St. Petersburg
16 June, 15:00	Finland	☐☐	Russia	St. Petersburg
17 June, 18:00	Denmark	☐☐	Belgium	Copenhagen
21 June, 21:00	Finland	☐☐	Belgium	St. Petersburg
21 June, 21:00	Russia	☐☐	Denmark	Copenhagen

Team	P	W	D	L	GD	Pts
1						
2						
3						
4						

GROUP C

13 June, 18:00	Austria	☐☐	N Macedonia	Bucharest
13 June, 21:00	Netherlands	☐☐	Ukraine	Amsterdam
17 June, 15:00	Ukraine	☐☐	N Macedonia	Bucharest
17 June, 21:00	Netherlands	☐☐	Austria	Amsterdam
21 June, 18:00	N Macedonia	☐☐	Netherlands	Amsterdam
21 June, 18:00	Ukraine	☐☐	Austria	Bucharest

Team	P	W	D	L	GD	Pts
1						
2						
3						
4						

GROUP D

13 June, 15:00	England	☐☐	Croatia	London
14 June, 15:00	Scotland	☐☐	Czech Rep	Glasgow
18 June, 18:00	Croatia	☐☐	Czech Rep	Glasgow
18 June, 21:00	England	☐☐	Scotland	London
22 June, 21:00	Croatia	☐☐	Scotland	Glasgow
22 June, 21:00	Czech Rep	☐☐	England	London

Team	P	W	D	L	GD	Pts
1						
2						
3						
4						

GROUP E

14 June, 18:00	Poland	☐☐	Slovakia	Dublin
14 June, 21:00	Spain	☐☐	Sweden	Bilbao
18 June, 15:00	Sweden	☐☐	Slovakia	Dublin
19 June, 21:00	Spain	☐☐	Poland	Bilbao
23 June, 18:00	Sweden	☐☐	Poland	Dublin
23 June, 18:00	Slovakia	☐☐	Spain	Bilbao

Team	P	W	D	L	GD	Pts
1						
2						
3						
4						

GROUP F

15 June, 18:00	Hungary	☐☐	Portugal	Budapest
15 June, 21:00	France	☐☐	Germany	Munich
19 June, 15:00	Hungary	☐☐	France	Budapest
19 June, 18:00	Portugal	☐☐	Germany	Munich
23 June, 21:00	Portugal	☐☐	France	Budapest
23 June, 21:00	Germany	☐☐	Hungary	Munich

Team	P	W	D	L	GD	Pts
1						
2						
3						
4						

ROUND OF 16

26 June, 21:00, Match 37, London

Winner Group A   Runners-up Group C

☐ v ☐

26 June, 18:00, Match 38, Amsterdam

Runner-up Group A   Runners-up Group B

☐ v ☐

27 June, 21:00, Match 39, Bilbao

Winner Group B   Third place Group A/D/E/F

☐ v ☐

27 June, 18:00, Match 40, Budapest

Winner Group C   Third place Group D/E/F

☐ v ☐

28 June, 18:00, Match 41, Copenhagen

Runners-up Group D   Runners-up Group E

☐ v ☐

28 June, 21:00, Match 42, Bucharest

Winner Group F   Third place Group A/B/C

☐ v ☐

29 June, 21:00, Match 43, Glasgow

Winner Group E   Third place Group A/B/C/D

☐ v ☐

29 June, 18:00, Match 44, Dublin

Winner Group D   Runners-up Group F

☐ v ☐

QUARTER-FINALS

2 July, 18:00, Match 45, Saint Petersburg

Winner Match 41   Winner Match 42

☐ v ☐

2 July, 21:00, Match 46, Munich

Winner Match 39   Winner Match 37

☐ v ☐

3 July, 18:00, Match 47, Baku

Winner Match 40   Winner Match 38

☐ v ☐

3 July, 21:00, Match 48, Rome

Winner Match 43   Winner Match 44

☐ v ☐

SEMI-FINALS

6 July, 21:00, Match 49, London

Winner Match 45   Winner Match 46

☐ v ☐

7 July, 21:00, Match 50, London

Winner Match 47   Winner Match 40

☐ v ☐

UEFA EURO 2020 FINAL

11 July, 21:00, London

☐ v ☐

Goalscorers   Goalscorers

Man of the Match:

Note: All kick-off times are CET (Central European TIme)

Picture Credits

ABOVE: Skillzy will be front and centre at UEFA EURO 2020.

The publishers would like to thank the following sources for their kind permission to reproduce the pictures in this book. (T-top, C-centre, B-bottom, L-left, R-right)

Getty Images: /AFP: 55; /Adem Altan/AFP: 38L; /Emilio Andreoli/UEFA: 24T, 74L; /Lars Baron/Bongarts: 102R; /Josef Bollwein/Sepa Media: 66R; / Simon Bruty: 69; /Geoff Caddick/AFP: 90L; /Jean Catuffe: 26T; /Reinaldo Coddou H. /UEFA: 52R; /Fabrice Coffrini/AFP: 23B, 44L, 44R, 45, 111; / Harold Cunningham/UEFA: 11, 34-35; /Alex Davidson: 106-107; /Oscar Del Pozo/AFP: 87; /Denis Doyle: 84R; /Thomas Eisenhuth: 78L, 78R, 79; / Paul Ellis/AFP: 108; /Franck Fife/AFP: 25B, 100R, 101; / Stu Forster: 43, 81; /Alex Grimm/UEFA: 7; /Bertrand Guay/AFP: 119; /Jack Guez/AFP: 25T, 64L, 64R; /Paul Harding/UEFA: 16C; /Oliver Hardt/ UEFA: 6, 48L, 48R; / Hollandfoto/iStock: 15T; / Andrej Isakovic/AFP: 62L; /Catherine Ivill/ AFP: 42R; /Jasper Juinen: 115; /Martti Kainulainen/ Lehtikuva/AFP: 51; /Attila Kisbenedek/AFP: 75, 97; /Ozan Kose/AFP: 38R; /Nikola Krstic/SNS Group: 77; /Jan Kruger/UEFA: 91; / Christopher Lee/UEFA: 8-9, 16T, 73; /Matthew Lewis/UEFA: 17T; /Alex Livesey: 14T; /Thomas Lohnes/UEFA: 13B; /Denis Lovrovic/AFP: 120; /Olga Maltseva/AFP: 10, 128; /Angel Martinez: 85; / Joosep Martinson/ UEFA: 60L; /Clive Mason: 113; /Charles McQuillan/ UEFA: 61, 90R, 123; /Mimadeo/iStock: 16B; /Jonathan Nackstrand/AFP: 86L, 86R, 110, 117; /Alex Nicodim/NurPhoto: 24B; /Oleg Nikishin: 54R; / Alex Pantling/UEFA: 17B; /Octavio Passos: 98L, 99; /Valerio Pennicino/ UEFA: 40R, 50L; /Popperfoto: 93; /Tullio Puglia/UEFA: 13T, 15B, 30-31, 67; / Cristina Quicler/AFP: 84L; /Andreas Rentz/Bongarts: 105; /Clive Rose: 72L; /STR/AFP: 39; /Genya Savilov/AFP: 98R; /Lukas Schulze/ UEFA: 72R, 102L, 103, 116; /Justin Setterfield: 22T; /Johannes Simon/ UEFA: 23T, 49, 54L; / Janek Skarzynski/AFP: 65, 88L; /Srdjan Stevanovic: 62R, 63, 76L, 76R, 96R; /Boris Streubel/UEFA: 14B; /Lukasz Szelag/AFP: 118; /Laszlo Szirtesi: 74R; / TF-Images: 89; /Bob Thomas Sports Photography: 57; /John Thys/AFP: 52L, 60R, 112; /Harry Trump: 42L; /Nicolas Tucat/AFP: 88R /Markku Ulander/ Lehtikuva/AFP: 50R; /VI Images: 53, 125; /Geoffroy van der Hasselt/AFP: 100L; /Levan Verdzeuli/UEFA: 66L; /Claudio Villa: 40L, 41, 109; /Sebastian Widmann/ UEFA: 20-21; /James Williamson/AMA: 26B. **Hungarian Football Federation:** 96L. **Offside Sports Photography:** /L'Equipe: 19, 33. **Sportsfile:** /Brendan Moran/UEFA: 17C, 22B, 121, 122

Every effort has been made to acknowledge correctly and contact the source and/or copyright holder of each picture any unintentional errors or omissions will be corrected in future editions of this book.